Motivational Marketing

Motivational Marketing

How to Effectively Motivate Your Prospects
to Buy Now, Buy More,
and Tell Their Friends Too!

ROBERT IMBRIALE

John Wiley & Sons, Inc.

M⌐

Published by John Wiley & Sons, Inc., Hoboken, New Jersey.
Published simultaneously in Canada.

Wiley Bicentennial Logo: Richard J. Pacifico

For general information on our other products and services or for technical support, please contact our Customer Care Department within the United States at (800) 762-2974, outside the United States at (317) 572-3993 or fax (317) 572-4002.

Wiley also publishes its books in a variety of electronic formats. Some content that appears in print may not be available in electronic books. For more information about Wiley products, visit our web site at www.wiley.com.

Library of Congress Cataloging-in-Publication Data:

Imbriale, Robert.
    Motivational marketing : how to effectively motivate your prospects to buy now, buy more, and tell their friends too! / Robert Imbriale.
        p.   cm.
    ISBN 978-0-470-11635-7 (cloth)
    1. Marketing—Psychological aspects.   I. Title.
    HF5415.I397   2007
    658.8'342—dc22

                                                        2007013501

Printed in the United States of America.

10 9 8 7 6 5 4 3 2 1

To the most amazing woman
a man could ever hope to find—
the love of my life, Phoebe.

I'm truly blessed by your incredible love
and undying support.
All the words in this book could not begin to express
how grateful I am that you chose
to be on this journey with me.
You make miracles possible.
Thank you for being all that you are.

CONTENTS

Chapter 14

Chapter 15

Chapter 16

FOREWORD

Freud's Second Question

The joke is that, with his dying breath, Sigmund Freud gasped a question implicit with an admission of ignorance: "Well, what DO women want, anyway?" Had he had but a few more breaths, his next and final question might have been: "Well, why DO people buy, anyway?"

Every businessperson, sales professional, and advertising copywriter should be endlessly exploring this second question. Sadly, few do. Instead, most stay stubbornly focused on the questions of: "How can we sell our *thing*?" and "How can we make them buy our *thing*?" And sadly, most sales training remains focused on selling. We are all better served pondering the psychology of the buyer rather than techniques and tactics of selling. That's what Robert Imbriale has done in *Motivational Marketing*.

Somewhere in this book, you'll find his answer to: *why people buy outrageously expensive Rolex watches, when a $40 Timex does the job.* Most people have knee-jerk, simplistic ideas about this. They chalk it up to ego or to the folly unique to those with more money to spend than they know what to do with. But there is a more complex answer with deeper meaning that is infinitely more useful to the astute marketer. I specifically recommend this part of the book to make you think about how the "why" of the Rolex buyer should be applied to your particular business. And I would add this quick point: You will be tempted to dismiss this, because "Your business is different." Since you sell custom-tooled machine parts to professional purchasing agents, tutoring services to parents, lawn service, carpet cleaning, life insurance, and so on, the "why people buy Rolex watches secret" is of no relevance to you. But you couldn't be more wrong. Recognizing what it does have to do with you, your clientele, and how you sell to them could make a million-dollar difference in your income. It could shower you with so much money that you can indulge in buying such luxuries as Rolex watches.

You might ask: Is there anything new here? I can't answer that, because what is old to one person is new to another and vice versa. When Robert invited me to provide this Foreword and I reviewed the manuscript, I hesitated—concerned that there wasn't enough new ground broken in these pages to warrant my endorsement (with which I am notoriously stingy). With a second and third reading, I found a handful of pages to mark, a handful of passages to highlight, not so much of new things but of things said differently, examples presented brilliantly, and insights into the individual's buying processes enunciated clearly. Had I purchased this book myself at the bookstore, this is more than enough for me. That is how I urge you to approach this book; look for the handful of things that "wake you up" about how you approach your advertising, marketing, and selling. Is it aimed from you toward your prospects, or is it drawn from inside your prospect's psyche? Certainly, the discussion of product-centered selling versus prospect-centered selling is *not* new. Good grief, it dates back to Elmer Letterman and Red Motley and J. Douglas Edwards and Robert Collier, into the 1920s and 1940s. But it is easy to forget, easy to drift from the correct place. It is easy to be *about* ourselves and our products instead of *about* our customers. This book is a valuable exercise in being about the customer.

Most businesspeople *think* they understand their customers' buying motives and criteria, but if pressed, they can only discuss it on a superficial level. They think their customers want quality, value, service, lowest prices, or ironclad guarantees. But there's no real leverage at this level. Every buyer wants these things; every seller must promise them; most do. We need to dig deeper—where Freud would dig—down to the deeper, earthier, more private and personal, even unconscious buying motives. As an example, I was involved in research that revealed the most important like/dislike about dental offices voiced by patients in probing interviews had nothing to do with the quality of the care, doctor's expertise, absence of pain from treatment, or price. The big "it" was about how they were greeted in the office. Patients hated being called out of the waiting room by a bellowing staff person seated behind a counter. Patients loved having a staff person come out into the waiting room, walk over to them, greet them, and escort them into the treatment rooms. The psychology here has to do with *respect*. What the patients wanted more than anything else was respect. In one of Robert's examples in this book, you discover why hobbyists buy craft supplies to glue shiny objects on gourds. It's not respect, but it is a single word that also starts with an R, and it is another deep psychological and emotional longing.

This book can help you dig deeper and get to an understanding of why *your* customers buy.

DAN S. KENNEDY

Dan S. Kennedy is the author of numerous business, marketing, and sales books including *No B.S. Direct Marketing for Non-Direct Marketing Business* and others in the No B.S. series, as well as *The Ultimate Marketing Plan* and *The Ultimate Sales Letter*. His books can be previewed at www.NoBSBooks.com. In addition, readers of this book may obtain Dan's "Greatest Free Gift Ever," including a free trial subscription to his *No B.S. Marketing Letter* at www.NoBSWebMarketing.com.

ACKNOWLEDGMENTS

To Laurie Harting, my editor at John Wiley & Sons, whose hard work has helped make this book the professional publication that it has become. Thank you, Laurie, I could not have done this without your guidance and support.

To Dan Kennedy, who has been instrumental in my marketing career as a mentor and friend. Dan, you're both a great mentor and inspiration of what can be done in the world of marketing.

To Anthony Robbins, who gave me the gift of understanding human emotion and how emotion affects the decisions we make in life. Thank you, Tony for seven great years of growth and contribution.

To my dad, for showing me that I was indeed a leader at heart and for always believing in me, no matter which path I chose to follow in life.

To Phoebe, who selflessly allowed me to forgo many household chores and responsibilities in favor of having the time to dedicate to writing this book. I could not have done it without your daily support. Thank you for being my soul mate, best friend, and life partner.

INTRODUCTION

Thank you for purchasing this book. In the coming pages, what you discover will change the way you market your business. What you read in this book may double, triple, or even quadruple the response to your advertising efforts, starting with the very next ad you place.

Yes, that's a big claim to make, and I know you may be a tad skeptical at the moment—that's perfectly normal. As you go through this book, you see how I apply motivational marketing to more than just advertising.

You'll read about specific companies that have benefited immediately from motivational marketing to the tune of millions and millions of dollars in additional income.

Before we get started, I'd like to share a brief history of *Motivational Marketing*'s development to help you understand that this book is more than some far-fetched idea I came up with one cold dark night.

Motivational Marketing has been more than a decade in development, and I've tested what I share with you in this book with thousands of companies in dozens of industries and the results have been nothing short of impressive.

IN THE BEGINNING

I didn't start out as a professional marketer, nor did I have the inclination to become one during my college years, but the industry became very appealing to me shortly after college. My first college degree was in commercial photography, not advertising or marketing, and it had nothing to do with writing marketing copy.

After college I found myself managing the largest commercial photo studio in New York City. I knew there was more out there for me, so I began to look around to see what else I could do with my life. Day after day, I watched as advertising executives came into the photo studio I managed to direct the photo shoots. During those shoots, I had no idea what the final ad would ultimately look like.

I was unfamiliar with that other side until the day I found my way out of the darkroom and into the bright lights of a Manhattan advertising agency.

There, I saw how the ads came together. I watched with incredible interest as highly paid people sat around and wrote not much more than a single sentence all day long—a sentence that would result in millions and millions of dollars in sales.

I asked myself how they knew which set of words would get people to buy what they were selling. How did they decide on just those five or seven words from the more than 60,000 in use in the English language everyday?

Not long afterward, I enrolled in an adult education class on marketing. At that time, I was concentrating on advertising and only heard the word *marketing* from time to time and never really knew its true meaning.

The first night of class, the professor asked the class to define marketing. I was quick to answer, "Selling!" Buzzzzzz! Sorry. Next!

Ouch, that hurt. When the professor finally explained what marketing was, it was some long-winded definition that really meant nothing to me or anybody else in that classroom.

So there I was learning about this thing called marketing, without knowing what it even was. It became my passion to find an easy way to define *marketing* since it seemed I was not the only one who didn't know how to explain it.

Today, I have a very simple, yet accurate definition of marketing. The rest of this book is directly related to marketing in the way that I define it.

THE DEFINITION OF MARKETING

Marketing is doing everything you can to make it *easy* for people to give you money in exchange for your goods and/or services.

So what is marketing? It's the smile on the face of the receptionist at the front desk; it's the way the phone is answered; it's the message you send in an e-mail, the copy on your web site, the headline in your sales letter, the ease of parking close to the entrance, a clearly lit and easy to understand sign, a company name that doesn't leave people wondering what you do, and so much more.

Our job, as marketers, is to do everything in our power to make it as easy as possible for people to give us their money in exchange for our goods and services.

The easier we make it to buy from us, the more sales we make. It's simple. But I can walk into any business and find barriers that get in the way of and often stop the buying process dead in its tracks!

Maybe the store wants to save a few dollars and doesn't get a merchant account and hence you can't buy from them with a credit card. That is just one example of a barrier to you doing business with them.

Think about your customer and consider how many barriers there might be in the way of people making a purchase from you. I find new ones in my own business all the time. The more I look, the more ways I find to make it easier for people to buy from me.

For instance, for years on my web site, www.UltimateWealth .com, I accepted credit cards as the preferred form of payment and never gave it another thought.

One day I was thinking about the person who may want to buy from me but either doesn't have a credit card or his money is in another account. That bit of insight came to me when I was trying to buy something online and realized my money was in another account and not on my credit/debit card. I was unable to make the purchase.

Seeing that, I immediately found a way to accept a check online, via fax, or in the mail. I also added the option to pay via PayPal. It was a revelation. This one small change made it easier for people to buy from me. Each one of these changes increased my web site sales by about 10 percent to 14 percent as soon as the change was implemented.

Ask yourself every day you're in business: "What can I do to make it easier for people to buy from my business?"

Motivational Marketing takes this concept to a whole new level and in this book, you're going to get my top motivational marketing strategies along with examples of how I've used them with my own businesses as well as with my many clients.

Motivational Marketing is designed to make it easier for people to buy from you by reaching them at an emotional level rather than just the logical level that so many marketers use in their promotional efforts.

In my first marketing position, I was hired by a direct mail pharmacy as their director of marketing. I lasted a mere 10 weeks in that position. Actually, I was let go because I completed in 10 weeks what the owner of the company expected would take me an entire year to complete.

During the rather short period of being director of marketing for the first time in my marketing career, I asked the question, "What could we do to make it easier for people to buy from us?"

I looked at what this company was doing and found a gaping hole in their marketing strategy. They spent large sums of money on advertising every month then sat back and waited for clients to call and place orders for their prescription drugs.

After asking questions and looking at what they were doing, I decided to create a simple one-page form that would be included with every order that was shipped out.

The form was an authorization form allowing us to automatically refill any recurring prescriptions every 30, 60, or 90 days. It was a great way to make it easier for our customers to buy from us again and again because they no longer had to worry about calling us each month to reorder the same prescription drugs.

After filling out this simple, one-page form, we'd simply auto-ship them their refill every 25 days so it would be in their hands just as their current supply was running out.

Did it work? The company saw a $20 million increase in bottom-line profits that year. This was the result of one sheet of paper that made it easier for their customers to do business with them.

While this is not what I today call *motivational marketing*, it was the foundation that began my career in marketing.

Following that experience, I was hired by an information marketing firm, again as the director of marketing. The issue this time was to help this company increase their sales by getting their prospects to correctly value the information they were buying.

It's easy enough for people to buy from you if you can clearly demonstrate to them the value you offer. But how do you do that?

Well, this company mailed (yes, paper in envelopes, with stamps) more than 50,000 brochures every week, attempting to sell their information reports. Sales at that time were about one sale for 1,000 pieces of mail sent out.

At that rate, the company was barely profitable, and I was hired to figure out what they could do to increase sales to maybe two sales per 1,000 pieces mailed. That would effectively double their business. The challenge was that if I failed to accomplish this goal, my job, and even the company might be gone forever.

The first step I took was to look long and hard at the entire operation. In this company, they had seven people working all week stuffing envelopes in a dark and stuffy mailroom. It was obvious they needed to change that situation because nobody stayed there very long and it was getting harder and harder to find people who would work in such dismal conditions.

There was no money to spend on marketing because they simply didn't have it to spend. This is very common with many businesses that see marketing as a high-risk proposition and not as an investment in the business.

While it's hard to remove all the risks associated with marketing, in this book, you're going to see how you can use motivational marketing to reduce your risks and increase the response to your marketing efforts.

When you're trying to figure out what's not working, try sending yourself the exact same mailing piece you're already sending to your prospects. This simple process will allow you to see the mailing piece in a completely new light and things will jump out at you. I did this and the next day I came home and sure enough there was an envelope in my mailbox from my company.

Now, I was just like the 50,000 other prospects who were getting this mailing each week in their mailboxes, piled in along with everything else. I asked questions like "Do I want to open this?" and "What do I expect to find inside?"

The first problem was that I immediately saw their envelope as a marketing piece trying to sell me something I wasn't sure I wanted! After opening the envelope, I found their brochure and nothing else.

Now if I didn't know what this company did, or wasn't in the market for their information, this brochure might as well have been written in Greek.

The challenges were many, but I was determined. First, we had to redesign the outside of the envelope. I simply added a small tag line under the company name that helped the recipient understand what we did.

Next, I created a sales letter to put into the envelope but there was not enough money to print it. We didn't even discuss the additional labor needed to stuff a second piece into each envelope effectively doubling the workload of that lowly mailroom.

The key was automation. I let five of the seven mailroom staff go and hired a company that commingled, presorted, stamped, and mailed the brochures for us. They were so efficient and cheap that I was able to reduce the size of the mailroom and save the additional rent we were paying for that space.

As a result, I had enough money to test my single-page sales letter. The results were astounding. Yes, I doubled the number of sales per thousand pieces mailed, and did much better than that.

Over the next six months, we averaged seven sales per 1,000 pieces mailed. I had cut the mailroom staff from seven to just two. I had relieved the company of paying rent for additional space, and I was able to cut the number of pieces mailed each week and increase sales in the process.

Was it the sales letter? Did that make it easier for people to buy? If it did anything it made it clear to the prospect *why* they needed the information we were offering.

They now saw the *value* of having our information reports and sales increased proportionately. This got me even more interested in the topic of why people buy. The interest ignited my passion for what I now call *motivational marketing*.

In my next job, I was the director of marketing for a firm that brokered mailing lists. I was considered an expert in the direct marketing world and now I would experience direct marketing from another perspective—the list rental side of the business.

Something was missing, but I wasn't sure what it was. I was writing sales letters and newsletters as well as beginning to sell online. At that time I was also writing sales copy for the electronic Bulletin Board System (BBS) that I had set up for this company.

What I knew was *how* to write copy that sold, but I had no idea *why* what I was writing worked or didn't work. Some days, I hit a home run and wrote a sales letter or display ad that worked very well and other days my writing didn't sell a thing.

It became somewhat frustrating for me because I love to get great results from my work and I didn't understand why some things worked as well as they did while other things simply didn't.

I wish I could say I hit multiple home runs as director of marketing for this company, but I didn't. My accomplishments were limited to increasing sales by only 30 percent a year for the two years I was with the company.

There was a piece missing, but I had no idea what it was.

A few months before I left my position at this company, I attended a seminar by somebody you may know, Anthony Robbins. Yes, it was a personal development seminar.

What I didn't know before I attended this first event was that Tony was all about teaching psychology. I had taken one psychology course in college and hated it because it was just so boring.

Tony made it fun, and I dug into his teachings in a big way. I eventually completed all of his programs and became a trainer with his company. Through every seminar, my thinking was focused on how I would apply what I was learning from Tony to my passion—marketing.

Making the connection was not long in coming. Tony has a unique way of showing you why people do what they do. I wanted to know why they opened one envelope and not another. Or why they bought a $25,000 Rolex watch, when a $40 Timex did the same job.

Or why some people spent their last dime on cigarettes instead of paying their landlord the rent they owed. I had questions and I wanted answers.

In the seven years I worked with Tony's organization, I coached thousands of people, I taught Tony's material in live seminars for one of his franchises, and I continued to build my marketing career, mostly online.

By paying close attention to my own feelings and emotions, and using the tools I learned from Tony, I started to get answers to my questions like what is it that really makes a person respond to a postcard, click a link in an e-mail message, or pick up the phone at 2:00 A.M. to order the "Super Crunch" exerciser.

The answers I had sought so long ago began to formulate. What I had learned from my own experiences early on and from what I was seeing and feeling now started forming what I now call *motivational marketing*.

Now, I have to be honest about something. It was never my intention to share this information publicly. By the time I first spoke about motivational marketing, it was at a live seminar and I had been using this method for more than five years.

The reason I never wanted to share it was because knowing how to motivate a person to buy is *an incredibly powerful tool*, and it can also be used to manipulate people to do or buy things they otherwise would not buy.

I appeal to your sense of morality when using the strategies I share with you in this book. Use them as much as you can in all your marketing, just think about what you're selling and be sure it offers true value to your customers.

Now you know the origins of motivational marketing, it's time to start unveiling the process of using it in your business to produce massive results.

As you read this book, you're going to notice that I use many examples from advertisers with big budgets and deep pockets. I do this because it's simply easier to illustrate the motivational marketing strategy to you.

By the end of this book, I promise to give you simple, low-cost, and no-cost alternatives that use the same motivational marketing techniques as the big guys. Even with a modest $20 per week budget, you'll be able to use most of what I'll share with you in this book.

Let's get started.

Motivational Marketing and Why It Is Important to Your Business

Nothing happens until a person is *motivated* by some force to take action. For example, before a person takes even the first step toward making a purchase, no matter how small it may be, he or she must be motivated.

Picture this in your mind: You're sitting at home on a warm summer day, enjoying time off from work, and doing nothing at this moment. You're simply enjoying the moment.

What would it take to get you to get dressed, get in your car, drive to the store, and buy something? You would need some form of motivation.

Let's say you're motivated by thirst. You suddenly realize that your day would be more joyful if only you could satisfy your thirst.

Motivated by the pain of thirst or the vision of satisfaction you'll experience once your thirst is quenched, you get up and walk over to the refrigerator only to find there's nothing to drink.

Now how do you feel? Did the motivation suddenly go away, or did it actually increase?

I'll bet now you're motivated by even more pain of having nothing to drink, or the even stronger vision of how good it would be to have a nice cold drink in your hands right now.

So you grab your wallet and keys, and you're off to the store.

On your way, you begin to think about what you're going to buy. You think about how you want to feel, but in your mind, you link that feeling to certain drinks you may have seen effectively advertised on television.

Will it be a popular cola, bottled water, or the latest energy drink? It all depends on how effectively the advertising from the company linked the product emotionally in your mind.

Think about a nice cold drink, outside, under the summer sun. What comes to mind?

You're probably going to buy that drink, or something similar, not because one contains more high fructose corn syrup, or more yellow number 5 than the other, but rather because of your perception of how that drink will make you feel.

So you're motivated by emotions—those the advertiser suggested you'd feel while drinking and enjoying their product.

You were motivated initially by thirst, then further motivated by advertising until finally you walked up to the checkout stand with a cool drink in your hand, happy, and ready to get back home for more rest and relaxation.

WHAT REALLY MOTIVATES PEOPLE TO BUY?

In our society, there are hundreds of motivations, but only a handful are really worth our attention as marketers. Throughout this book, I share the top five *emotional motivators* and show you decisively how to integrate them into your marketing materials.

These five emotional motivators have the power to get somebody off the couch, into his car, to your store, and further to convince him to purchase the exact product you want him to, without ever so much as noticing the competition.

❧ SUCCESS STRATEGY ❧

Nothing is sold until you can motivate people to make a purchase. Motivation is what makes people take action.

In my role as a marketing consultant, I always look to the emotions that motivate people to buy the products and services my clients sell. If I could get inside prospects' heads, I would want to know the answers to the following questions:

- ✔ What are they thinking?
- ✔ What are they feeling?
- ✔ What emotions could I use in my marketing to motivate them to buy now?

When you have the answers to these questions, you can build a marketing system that works reliably for years on end.

The emotional motivators in this book have not changed since the day people started to market. Neither will they change any time in the future because people have always been motivated by the same primary driving emotions.

Our job, as marketers, is to find out what those emotions are and appeal to them in every ad, every sales letter, web page, radio spot, or infomercial we create. I go even further and tap into those same emotions by adding text on the outside of an envelope, on order forms, on the letter I send along with the product they've already bought and paid for, and on the product itself.

MOTIVATION IS A CONTINUOUS PROCESS

The key to motivational marketing is to do everything you can to motivate your prospects to buy from you and to keep them motivated during and even after the buying process is complete.

It's been said that motivation is like bathing. It feels great when you take a bath, but it doesn't last. Soon enough you'll be ready for another bath, then another—throughout your entire lifetime.

Because motivation is not long lasting, we have to constantly motivate our prospects to buy from us again and again.

Your goal is to motivate your prospect before and during the buying process, as well as after the product arrives. If the buyer remains motivated about her purchase, you remove the possibility of buyer's remorse, cut refunds to the bare minimum, and increase the likelihood that your buyer will actually use your product or service.

There are two of types of people who buy from your business. The first is simply a *good customer*. These are the customers who come back repeatedly to buy from you without much effort on your part to sell to them.

The second, preferred type of customer is called a *raving fan*. Think back to your days as a teenager who was so excited about the latest sci-fi movie you saw that you could not wait to tell your friends—now you know what I mean.

Raving fans not only support your business but also help it grow. When you can keep fans motivated, they will spread the word about your offering or product to their circles of influence. The word spreads and you end up with more and more customers.

This is the power of motivational marketing. In my world, I go even farther with the motivational concept to make sure the people who work with my company are motivated and excited to work with us.

People who aren't excited about what we're creating take the rest of the team down. I make sure anybody who is not motivated is replaced immediately.

If this sounds harsh, it is—on the front end. On the back end, it's better for everybody if the business has a motivated team working together.

Motivation is the fuel that makes a business run or a person buy from you. Without that fuel, sales aren't made and soon the business will close its doors forever.

Master what you read in these pages and I promise you the business you build will be one that allows you to live the life of your dreams.

Now, let's look at the first important information you must clearly understand to properly use motivational marketing in your business.

CHAPTER

Motivate Your Prospects to Buy Now

There is a common belief that to have a successful business you go out and *find a need and fill it.*

While that's not completely wrong, a better way to have a successful business is to find an emotional want and then satisfy that want with your products and services.

Think about something you bought for yourself in the past three to five days. It can be anything from a soft drink to a new car or a house. What you bought really doesn't matter.

Now ask, "Why did I buy this item?"

UNDERSTANDING WANTS VERSUS NEEDS

If you're honest with yourself, you'll find that you most likely bought the item because you "wanted" it. I know, you're going to tell me how much you really "needed" it and that's why you bought it. Let's look a little deeper.

On the outside, you might think you made this particular purchase because you had a need to fill. You're not entirely wrong.

You and I do buy the things we "need" at the market. That's where this can get a little confusing at first. Hang in there. When you get this point, it will completely transform your business.

While we do buy products we "need," there are many different choices for what amounts to essentially the same product.

Think about this distinction: You may think you buy the things you need, but the decision to actually buy a particular product is really based on what you *want*. Understanding this will help you use motivational marketing in the most effective way possible.

Think about the last time you went to the store to buy toothpaste. Everyone needs toothpaste. But if need were the only driving force, *any* brand of toothpaste would do, right?

So why are there dozens of brands on the market? Why does the same company offer so many different choices? After all, our need is simply to have a clean mouth. Honestly, a scoop of baking soda would suffice, yet we spend billions of dollars each year on all kinds of fancy toothpaste.

The companies that make toothpaste also spend billions of dollars in advertising to get you to buy their brand and not the competition's brand. So which toothpaste do you buy?

We buy the brand we *want* based on what we *feel* it will do for us. This is what I call an *emotional want*.

One brand offers "minty fresh" breath. That's appealing to you if you're going on a date or to an important meeting. Imagine how you would feel if you whispered to your date and she nearly passed out due to your bad breath! You can't allow that, so you buy the toothpaste that promises you'll never have to feel worried about how your breath smells.

Another brand offers you whiter teeth. Whiter teeth, you're told in the advertising, will give you more self-esteem so that you'll feel more confident. If you want to feel more confident and believe the claim, this is the brand you'll buy.

Then there are those brands that offer it all in the same tube. This is for the person who wants the best of all worlds but doesn't want to brush seven times a day.

There are different brands of the same product on the market because people want to feel different things. The only way to cater to a diverse market is to have a diverse product line.

And it doesn't end there. No matter how small or how large the purchase, we buy what we want.

Think about purchasing a house. If I wanted to buy a house and contacted a real estate agent, when he took me to see a house, what would he say to me?

Would the agent tell me how thick the cement slab is under the house? Or how much rebar was used to support the driveway? I doubt he would even know that kind of information.

Instead, I'll be taken through the house and asked questions like:

- ✔ Would you prefer to put your home office in this room, or the one with the big, bright window?
- ✔ Where would you put your television?
- ✔ On which side of the garage would you park your car?

These kinds of questions have nothing to do with the home. Instead, they are designed to appeal to my emotions and to literally "put me in the house and make it my home" even before I move in.

The questions the agent asks are more about finding out my wants than they are about anything else:

- ✔ Do you want a two-car garage?
- ✔ Do you want a pool and spa?
- ✔ Do you want three bedrooms?
- ✔ Do you want two acres of land?

✔ Do you want an avocado grove?

✔ Do you want citrus fruit trees or oak trees?

They never ask you what you need. If they did, you'd find out that a straw shack would satisfy many of your needs, but it probably wouldn't make you very happy.

So from the smallest to the largest purchases we make, we buy the things we want, not the things we need. Emotional wants are a powerful motivator and it's what makes motivational marketing such a great marketing tool.

Whatever it is we want, we find a way of getting it. What we want is usually a feeling—and typically one of satisfaction and happiness.

PEOPLE BUY ON EMOTION AND JUSTIFY WITH LOGIC

People do what they do so that they feel a certain emotion that they really want to feel. Then they turn around and justify their decisions with logic.

While most people think only in terms of making decisions that are logical, that's not how decisions are made. They are made from emotion, then simply justified with "logic."

I put the word logic in quotes because I'm sure, like me, you've heard many very unique logical reasons for the purchases people make. Some are enough to make your head spin.

It's important to understand that the decisions people make are primarily emotional decisions and rarely, if ever, based on logic. The logic is added later.

It's next to impossible to share in words what you are feeling about the decisions you make, so we human beings look for the more concrete logical reasons to justify our decisions to ourselves and to others.

How would I explain to you why I really bought the house I now live in? Can I tell you how the space made me *feel*? Even if I tried, you'd look at me and ask yourself if a smaller house could have done the same thing for me?

After all, what more do you need in life than a place to sleep, watch television, and cook some food? Do you really need a huge living area? Or the Koi pond? The guest house? The sound studio? People don't need those things—but they may want the feeling that those things provide.

Does a person really *need* a $24,000 Rolex watch or will a $40 Timex do the same job? It's not logic, it's emotion.

How does wearing that Rolex make you feel? Like a millionaire!

What will people think of you if you walk in the room with a shiny new Rolex on your wrist? How will they treat you? This is why people buy Rolex watches. They don't need them because they keep better time. People buy Rolexes because of the way they feel when they wear one.

I could find many product examples like this. Whatever you buy is bought because of the way it makes you feel. This is equally true of the big stuff, and the small stuff we buy.

Isn't the same true of people who get married? They get married because of how they think it will feel to be married to that special person. Today, we don't get married for the logical reasons used in generations past.

Some of the biggest decisions a person makes in his or her life are made for emotional reasons and then only later are they justified with logic.

The most interesting aspect of this process is that people can justify *anything*.

Think about it. What was the logical justification for that product you clearly bought for emotional reasons? I'm sure you can think of hundreds of these purchases in just the past year alone.

From a marketing perspective, you want to engage your prospect's emotions and at the same time you want to be sure the logical reasons for making the purchase are there too. Remember, marketing is about making it easy for your prospects to give you money in exchange for your products and services.

You know your customers are buying on emotion, but they will still have to justify their purchase with themselves and with others later on. Make it easy by giving them both the emotional and the logical reasons for buying from you now.

The challenge for you as a motivational marketer is to resist the temptation to focus all your marketing efforts on the logical reasons for your prospects to buy from you.

This is where you'll get into trouble and it's where most marketers miss the boat. During the first years of my marketing career, I wrote sales letters, fax broadcasts, postcards, and newsletters all focused only on the logical reasons of buying what I was selling.

As I began to understand that people use their emotions to make a buying decision, my entire method for marketing changed. I've gone back to look at some of my early sales letters and it's almost comical to see how devoid of emotion they were.

Pay attention to your conversations with family, friends, and associates. What you'll find is that you speak mostly in terms of logical reasons to justify what it is you do and what you hope to do, be, or buy.

If I were speaking to a friend about buying a new BMW, my conversation would revolve around things like the car's great track record, how well they cover repairs, and how reliable these cars are. I might speak about the car's awesome power, ability to accelerate quickly, and safety record.

All are logical reasons why I might buy that car.

If I were honest, I would be talking about how great it would feel to be behind the wheel of the "Ultimate Driving Machine." I'd talk about what people would think of me when I show up in that car; and I'd speak about how much more re-spect I might feel from my clients.

In your marketing, you want to make sure you offer both the emotional and the logical in all of your marketing materials.

❧ SUCCESS STRATEGY ❧

Emotion is what moves people to decision. Although we think in terms of logic, it's our emotions that weigh in most when it comes time to make a decision.

The more you tap into your prospects' emotional wants, the more they will respond to your advertising, and the more they will buy what you're selling.

Here's a key to making this work: Go all the way.

When I show my clients how to use emotion in their mar-keting, and they finally start to apply it to their own businesses, they tend to do so gingerly. They may tap lightly on emotional motivators, using only one. And they often fear emotional stuff altogether, as many people do in our society.

Many of us want nothing to do with emotional stuff, not be-cause we don't feel emotion, but more because of what society has taught us. For example, men are not men unless they are like steel and have total control over their emotions. The truth lies somewhere else.

Men do have emotions and they get excited, sad, motivated, angry, upset, empowered, happy, and so on. Although they feel all the same emotions as women, they have been taught to hide them.

When I speak with a male client about adding emotion into their marketing process, they can often be a little less than en-thusiastic at first.

Personal note to men only: If you're a man reading this, re-member, I'm a man writing this and it's okay for you to work with emotion in your life. I know you and I have been taught differently growing up, but listen, since so few of us men ever play with emotions in our work, think about how much *power* you'll have when you do. Trust me on this.

Now that everyone is on board with the idea of using emotion in marketing, the correct way to use emotion in marketing is to hit emotional motivators, and hit them hard.

It makes no sense to lightly tap an emotional motivator in your marketing efforts because that will not produce your desired results. What does make sense is to hit those emotional motivators with as much punch as you can possibly muster.

This is how you get people to respond emotionally to your marketing message. Keep this in mind as you explore the rest of this book and discover each of the most powerful emotional motivators.

Let's look at how to apply the emotional motivators to your marketing.

CHAPTER 3

Taking Aim at Your Prospect's Emotions

B ecause people buy based on their emotional wants, not their needs, your job is to come up with as many emotional wants as you possibly can.

When I teach the following information in a live seminar, I ask participants to list as many emotional wants as they can within a short 12-minute time period. Once they've exhausted their ideas, I share the next step—which gives them *immediate access* to hundreds of emotional wants that most likely did not come to mind.

Imagine the power you'd have if you could tap into hundreds of different emotional wants all linked to your product or service. Would it give you many more options when it came to creating your marketing copy? Would it open doors into new markets for you? You bet it would. Let's examine how.

A correctly linked emotional want is based on a benefit that your product or service offers the person who will ultimately buy and use what you're selling. When I was new to the marketing world, I confused the *benefits* and the *features* of whatever it was I was selling.

I'd create sales copy around the features of a particular product and miss mentioning the benefits altogether. Let me give you a typical example, one that I see very often with my clients and seminar participants.

In the mid-1990s, I worked for a real estate investment company who prepared a new program targeting real estate agents. The idea was that the real estate agents would make referrals to this real estate investment company and would share in a regular sales commission when the company bought a referred property. What made this offer different is that they would also get a piece of the increased selling price once the referred property was renovated and later resold.

I totally missed the boat in marketing this one. We planned a 10,000-piece direct mail campaign to real estate agents in New York, New Jersey, and Connecticut. My role was to write the sales letter for this promotion, and I was paid a commission on all the resulting sales. Obviously, I had plenty of motivation to make this promotion a real winner.

The sales letter I wrote reflected every tiny, tiny feature of the program we were offering. I even told the reader that they'd get a stack of business cards, and that we'd process their referrals within 24 hours of receiving them.

Never once in that letter did I touch on the benefits for the prospects. The letter focused on what was most important to the owners of the real estate investment company, but it had nothing to do with what was important to the people we were writing to.

When I showed my client the sales letter I had written, he loved it. The letter detailed every aspect of the program—how it worked, and what it included—but I left the rest up to the reader. Why did my client love the letter so much? It was all about what was important to him. He too missed the point that what was important to us was not important to the reader of this letter.

What was the result? Zero. Not one call, not one fax, nothing in the mail. It was a total waste of time, paper, postage, and labor. It hurt. A lot of money was invested in this project. I remember the day I took my $19,000 check for writing this sales letter to the bank. It really felt great.

When the letter failed to produce a single sale, I ended up giving back a large portion of the consulting fee that I had worked so hard to obtain.

But, as in all things that go dramatically wrong, I looked for the lessons. No matter what events happen in your life, they can all teach you something. Your job is to find the lessons, learn them, leave the pain behind, and move on.

When I found out what I had missed in writing that sales letter, I literally felt sick to my stomach. But I also knew I would never let it happen again.

Here's what I discovered: I had no clue why benefits were so critical to a marketing message.

I needed to find a simple, *memorable* way to differentiate features and benefits. After all, I expected to write many sales letters during my career and I certainly did not want to repeat that experience ever again.

Here's what I came up with and now use all the time when creating any marketing piece.

Features are about the *product*.

Benefits are about the *prospect*.

Anything that directly describes the product is a feature. For instance, if you describe the finish, color, or texture of your product, that's a feature. If you talk about the level of horsepower, amps, watts, capacity, duration, or strength, these too are all features.

Although these things can be very exciting to you if you're the creator of the product, they are of little value when marketing your product. Here's why.

You cannot ever leave it up to your prospects to make the translation from a feature to a benefit. That's your job and you do it in your marketing message.

Let me give you a simplistic example. Let's say you're selling a lawnmower that happens to be 5 horsepower (HP), red, and finished with a glossy coat of paint.

If you were the maker of this lawnmower, seeing that red machine might make you very excited because it's your creation. It may represent the culmination of years of research and millions of dollars in investments to make it a reality. This is your pride and joy.

If you were to do your own marketing, you'd promote the lawnmower's features from a place of pride and it would be reflected in your marketing. I wrote that horrible sales letter for my real estate investment client when I got caught up in what it took to create the program and dropped the ball when it came to translating features into benefits for the person reading the sales letter.

It happens. I sometimes catch myself doing the same thing with my products to this day. The difference is that now I can go back and correct it before I post it to a web site or send out any kind of marketing piece.

Your job as a marketer is to make it easy for people to buy what you're selling. You have to find out how the features of a product can be translated into becoming a true benefit to the person who will buy from you.

This process is so critical that if you miss it, everything else you do in your marketing will ultimately fail. Pay attention to the benefits!

Let's get back to the lawnmower. If I were going to sit down and write marketing copy in the form of a sales letter, sales flyer, television ad, web site, or direct mail piece, I would also start with a list of the three main features.

Let's take the first one: the 5 HP motor.

A marketer who has never purchased a lawnmower before may not have any frame of reference for what a 5 HP feature really means. In all likelihood, she'd look at that feature, shake her head, and move on to the next feature.

That's what most people would do. However, if I were writing the marketing copy, I might write about how a 5 HP lawnmower is one of the most powerful of all gas-powered mowers and, with this much power, you'd never have to worry about stalling this mower even in the tallest grass-cutting situation.

I'd talk about how at 5 HP, this motor will give you more years of useful life than a lower-powered machine, and how much faster you'll have a golf-course-like lawn with much less effort.

I could go on and on here, but you get the idea. I've taken a feature that is of little value to anybody but the manufacturer and turned it into a series of benefits that will reach a large part of the targeted market.

Second, why is it red? What if I don't like red and it only comes in red? What *benefit* is there to having a red mower?

As a marketer, you have to answer these questions with true benefits. You might state that passersby will see the bright red color and keep out of harm's way.

Or you might suggest that red is this year's hot color for mowers and, with a red mower, people will think you're really successful because you can afford the latest mower for your lawn.

Last, I'd look at the glossy finish coat on the mower. Why is that important to me, as your customer, I would ask.

What if this glossy coat would protect your mower from spilled gasoline, and would repel cut grass from sticking to the mower so that it will continue to look shiny and new for years to come?

The glossy finish coat really matters to me as a potential buyer of this mower. It may push me so far over the top that I would not even consider another mower that did not have a glossy coat finish!

If you knew the importance of the finish to the customer, you'd do all you could to promote your glossy coat finish, especially if your competitors didn't have a similar coating on their mowers.

You want to look at every feature and translate it into a true benefit that your prospects will identify with and that will help them make a buying decision. When you do this, you'll find your marketing becomes effortless and incredibly effective.

Personally, I list the features a product or service offers and translate each one into as many benefits as I can think of.

In the case of the lawnmower, I would write "5 HP" at the top of a blank page because that is one of the features of this particular product. Then, I'd fill the page with as many benefits that relate to this mower having a 5 HP motor as I could.

I may need to do some research, call a few landscape professionals, read some customer comments and feedback, or maybe even contact some past and current customers to ask them about this feature and its benefits for them.

Remember, I'm translating a feature into real benefits that appeal to a wide audience. If I only listened to my own thoughts, or looked at my own experiences, I'd end up with a very short list of benefits to work with. After all, the last time I remember pushing a lawnmower was when I was 16 years old.

TYPES OF BENEFITS

There are two types of benefits that you can use in your marketing. One of them is obvious, the other isn't. Yet it's this second type of benefit that is used most often in the marketing world to promote just about anything you can think of.

The first type of benefit is a "cause and effect" benefit that I call a *direct benefit*. This means that by owning or using a product, you get this benefit directly from the product or service you buy.

Let's say I'm selling a bottle of diet pills. What happens when you take diet pills? You lose weight (i.e., if the pills actually do what they advertise).

You could look at this direct benefit in this way: *take the pills, lose the weight.*

It's a true benefit, but is it really sexy? It would be if your diet pill was the only one on the market, but it's not. There are hundreds of brands available on the market, and they all claim that if you take their pills, you'll lose weight. It would be impossible to sell a diet pill that did not make this claim. Not a single brand on the market today omits this benefit.

They use it, but they also know it's going to take more than this one direct benefit to sell more diet pills. This is where the second type of benefit comes into play, and where you can make an ordinary product sexy.

This second kind, an *indirect benefit,* means that secondary things happen as a result of using your product or services. You get the direct benefit, plus a bonus—an indirect benefit. You could think of this as a side effect, only in a positive way.

Here is where you can have some fun because indirect benefits open up vistas of possibility for you as a marketer.

Let's go back to our bottle of diet pills. A direct benefit of taking the pills is that you lose weight. That is ho-hum and boring, actually.

You take the pills and lose the weight. We can't change this outcome because that's what the pills are designed to do, but what else happens when you lose the weight? What is an indirect benefit of taking these pills? Now we can get creative.

You might say a person who loses weight will also change other aspects of his life in the process. Maybe once he loses the weight, he finds he has more physical energy and increased stamina.

These are some of the indirect benefits for the user of a bottle of diet pills, but do the benefits end there? Of course they don't! Now that a person has more energy, what else might that lead to? Maybe he takes up sports, applies for a more physical job, spends more time playing with his kids, or keeping up with his more active spouse.

The processional effects of taking diet pills can literally go on and on. Here's a short list of indirect benefits from taking diet pills:

- ✔ Increased self-esteem.
- ✔ More confident.
- ✔ More outgoing.
- ✔ Meet the love of his/her life.
- ✔ Live longer.
- ✔ Dramatic improvements in level of health.
- ✔ Job promotion.
- ✔ More social.
- ✔ Able to fit into better-looking clothes.
- ✔ Get noticed more in public.
- ✔ More smiles from others.
- ✔ Easier time fitting in socially.
- ✔ More strength.
- ✔ Increased stamina.

I could literally create dozens and dozens of indirect benefits from one bottle of diet pills. Our job as marketers is to make it easy for our prospects to see exactly why they must buy what we're selling.

Using indirect benefits is a great way to accomplish this goal.

Let's go back to our example of the lawnmower. To make the purchase of this mower a little sexier, I used mostly indirect benefits in my example. If I just looked at direct benefits alone, I'd say, "Buy the mower, cut your grass." That is not too sexy.

Instead, I looked at the indirect benefits and soon had a few that were really sexy:

✔ Get the job done in half the time, with half the effort.

✔ Your lawn will look like a championship golf course.

✔ Have a great-looking, bright red machine for years to come.

✔ Grass won't stick to this glossy red finish, so you'll never have to wash this mower.

What I did was look at the features offered by this mower first, and then I made the translation into indirect benefits that would motivate a prospect to buy.

In the coming chapters, as I show you the top five emotional motivators, remember that you want to do all you can to use all five of them in every ad, sales letter, radio spot, television ad, or web site you ever create.

You may not see how each one applies to your product or service, but when you begin to explore the world of indirect benefits, you'll find it much easier to match an indirect benefit to an emotional motivator.

When I first began to use the emotional motivators, I, too, struggled to see how to get all of them into the same marketing piece. Many times, I gave up in frustration because there was nothing I could think of that would make them all fit.

That was before I understood the power of indirect benefits and how they open up whole new vistas of possibility for us. Now, I'm hard-pressed to find something that I can't fit into the five emotional motivators.

THE POWER OF FIVE

In my business, I write a lot of articles and many of them are published in the largest business magazines in the world. When I was first doing my research on the topic of motivational marketing, I began to look at a lot of advertising. I went through hundreds of magazines looking at ads that would either prove or disprove my motivational marketing theories.

I was lucky enough to have an entire year of a particular magazine in my possession because they had published 12 of my articles and had sent me copies of the magazine each month. What I found interesting was that there were plenty of ads in this magazine; some ads used emotional motivators, and some did not.

I began to tear out pages from all 12 issues of this magazine and place them in separate piles. One pile had ads that did not use emotional motivators, while the other pile had ads that used one or more emotional motivators.

Interestingly, the ads that used one or more of the emotional motivators were in the magazine month after month. I took careful notice of these ads.

To the contrary, the ads that did not use any of the emotional motivators were only in the magazine once and rarely showed up a second time. This was a clear sign the ads did not work as expected.

However, I did not look at the tiny classified ads. I focused my attention on half-page and full-page ads only. In this particular magazine, the cost to run a full-color, full-page ad was about $35,000 per insertion. That meant that every time the ad appeared in the magazine, the company behind the ad may have spent as much as $35,000.

This is a lot of money for a company to invest in an ad, so it had better produce results or it won't be in the next magazine issue. It was easy to track what was working and what wasn't. The ads that appeared month after month worked; those that were sporadic or only appeared once, didn't work.

This exercise proved by a wide margin that using emotional motivators works, but that using *more than one* of the emotional motivators at once is even more important. Some of the best ads I found used all five emotional motivators in the same ad.

If you don't use any of the emotional motivators in your advertising, you will probably fail to get the results you hoped for.

You're probably selling using logical reasons to a market that responds emotionally. Or you're running an ad filled with features (logic) and no benefits (emotion).

Emotional ads are abundant in the marketplace. Magazines have plenty of ads that are filled with emotional motivators, and ads that show up week after week, month after month, year after year do so because they work.

What's even more impressive are ads that have one, two, three, four, or even all five emotional motivators at work in the same ad. This is important because, in any target market, there are people who will respond to different emotional stimulus.

Just because an ad hits one emotional button does not mean that everybody in your target market is going to respond. That's why it's important to fit all five emotional motivators into the same ad or marketing piece. While it's not always possible to do so, I work hard to include all five in every marketing piece I create, either for myself or my clients.

There are companies out there who are experts at getting all five emotional motivators in each piece they create. These are the ads you want to study and mimic. You'll typically find these companies in multilevel marketing or network marketing.

You'll find that these network marketing companies grow the fastest as compared with other companies. While most network marketing companies are in and out of business inside of three years, those that use emotional motivators in their advertising last five or more years.

When they do it right, they hit all the emotional buttons, and hit them hard; they also tend to spend much more money on their advertising. The result is a company that grows exponentially in a very short period of time and outlasts all the others in the marketplace.

By appealing to more than one emotional button, they are able to capture a much larger audience and get them excited about buying their products. Many then go on to become part of the company. Study what they do and model it for your own business because it works.

Invest a few hours one day at your local library. Go to the periodicals section and pull out a year's worth of magazines such as *Entrepreneur* or *Home Business Magazine.* These magazines have advertisers that routinely run full-page ads that make great pieces for you to study.

Look for the full-page, full-color ads that are in the magazine month after month. Typically, the ads you find will be for network marketing companies or companies offering distributorships.

Take note of companies with full-page ads that use emotional motivators. Make color copies of all of these ads to study. Use them as a model when creating your own advertising.

You can create most anything using the indirect benefits your product or service offers. Your job is to find enough indirect benefits so that you can use every one of the emotional motivators in your marketing materials.

Although you're wondering what these emotional motivators are, I really needed you to have this foundation before we cover them because you may not immediately see how to apply them to your marketing. That's normal.

However, it's now time to dig into the core of motivational marketing. When you master the next five chapters, you'll be able to tap into a prospect's emotional reasoning. Think of each topic as a button you can press in your marketing materials that will cause a prospect to respond emotionally.

These buttons are called *emotional motivators.* It's one thing to use logic in your marketing materials, but when you use the five emotional motivators, you'll see an immediate and dramatic increase in response.

An entire chapter is dedicated to each emotional motivator because it is important that you clearly understand each emotional motivator and how to apply it to your marketing.

Let's look at the first of the five emotional motivators that make up the foundation of motivational marketing right now!

Emotional Motivator 1— Fear

The first of the five emotional motivators is *fear*. You may be familiar with the term *fear marketing*. This is where the marketer attempts to scare prospects into making an immediate buying decision.

To understand the power of fear to motivate people, you may want to think about the things that you fear. Maybe you have a fear of flying, spiders, or speaking on the telephone. Perhaps the thought of standing before an audience has your knees knocking with fear.

We all have fears. Most people deal with their fears by trying to forget about them. After all, how could you manage if you constantly thought about the things that made you afraid.

We bury our fears, and we do all we can to avoid situations where we might ever need to face the things we fear. Some people drive cross-country for days at a time because they fear getting on an airplane.

Other people refuse to venture into their backyards because they may see a spider, so they stay inside where they perceive it to be safe.

If you can connect a prospect with her greatest fear, and then position your product or service as a way to alleviate her fear, the prospect will buy from you.

If your prospect has a fear of spiders and you offer a solution that rids his home and yard of spiders, he is much more likely to buy from you now.

If there is a large crowd of people gathered and somebody yells, "FIRE!" the crowd is suddenly motivated to get out of there because they fear the fire or what the fire might do to them.

Using fear as a motivator in your marketing will have the same effect, and that is why so many marketers today use fear as their primary marketing strategy.

I'm not a big fan of using fear to a large extent in my marketing because people are already scared enough. I don't need to add to their fear with my marketing.

USING FEAR IN YOUR MARKETING MATERIALS

An effective method of using of fear to sell is to show your prospects what would happen to them if they did not buy your product or service. What would they miss or not have access to?

When I use fear marketing in that way, it's a powerful tool to motivate the person who is on the fence about making a buying decision.

For many years, it was commonly known in the marketing industry that you could not sell protection or security. It is true that you can't sell something that people do not have a current need for, and protection and security are not of interest unless there is a present and current threat that your prospect is motivated to solve now.

To overcome this marketing challenge, marketers have resorted to using fear tactics to get their prospects to respond and buy. They bring into the present what might happen sometime in the future.

In the world of neuro-linguistic programming (NLP), this process is known as "future pacing." This is very powerful because it takes a person from where they are today to where they could end up years from now unless they change something.

A very powerful, yet graphic, example of this is to take a young person to a hospital to see patients who suffer from the later stages of lung disease caused by a lifetime of smoking. This is not a pretty sight and if you tell this child how these people ended up here, the likelihood of her ever taking up smoking is low. This experience instills fear in the mind of that child and it motivates her to take the desired action of staying away from cigarettes. Remember, the bigger the fear, the more powerful the motivation.

You want to be able to do the same thing in your marketing. It does not have to be that graphic or scary. The fear you choose could be as simple as saying, "Place your order by Friday at noon, or you'll miss out on this special offer forever!"

Most of the marketing that I'm involved in uses the fear of missing a great opportunity, and not the more graphic kind just mentioned. This is very powerful and very necessary in all your marketing materials.

This technique is commonly called *scarcity marketing*, and it's based on the fear of missing out on something that you're offering. As you plan your next marketing piece, think about how you can limit your offer either by time, quantity, or some other factor.

A simple example might be to say your offer is available to just the first 250 people to respond. After that, your offer is no longer valid or the price goes back to the regular price.

You could limit your offer by time and say that your offer is valid only until a certain day or for the next 24 hours. These are very effective marketing strategies that do result in motivating people to respond now.

The fear of missing something great is a powerful tool that you must find ways to incorporate in all of your marketing pieces.

INCREASING FEAR

Maybe you want take things to a new level and use a little more fear in your marketing. Well, you certainly can and you see examples of this very often in the insurance industry, especially in the area of life insurance.

They might ask you a question such as, "What would happen to your family if you were suddenly killed?" That question sends chills down your spine because it's designed to do so. Then the advertiser will position its insurance offering as the solution to this chilling situation so that you can put your fears to rest.

One of the main reasons I've resisted using this level of fear in my own marketing is because people are scared and shocked all the time. Watch 10 minutes of any newscast and you'll see plenty of reasons to feel fear.

WHAT YOUR MARKET FEARS MOST

The key to making fear work in your marketing is to do your homework on your market. It would not serve you to create an ad that uses the fear of spiders as the main emotional motivator if only a small segment of your market has that fear and if your product or service offering has nothing to do with alleviating a fear of spiders.

In every market, there is a fear, or set of fears, that is shared by a large percentage of your prospects. If you have a solution to even one of those fears, you can tap into that fear and use it in your marketing materials.

To find this fear element, you may want to begin by looking at your product or service and ask yourself the following question: Does it alleviate a problem that may cause your prospect to experience pain either now or in the future?

A great example of this is a fire extinguisher. This is one of those products that falls into the category of protection. It's not sexy, and most people will walk right by and not notice them on store shelves.

When we ask what pain a fire extinguisher might alleviate, it's a pain that may happen in the future. As a marketer, your job would be to bring that future pain into the present, otherwise you'll never sell a single fire extinguisher.

What pain could your fire extinguisher alleviate for your prospects? Perhaps one of the biggest fears of all is losing everything you own to a fire that destroys your home. But buying a fire extinguisher is not on our minds on a daily basis, nor is it on most to-do lists.

Is it a fear? You bet it is! Is a fire possible? Sure, it is. Is it a fear that's on your mind today? Probably not. It's one of those fears we tend to file away and not pay any attention to until the moment something goes wrong and flames break out in our house.

It's too late by then. You can yell and scream all you want, but if you didn't buy a fire extinguisher, your chance of losing everything in the next 30 minutes is very real.

As a marketer, you want to bring this fear to the present moment and there are many tools you can use to do that.

You could interview a person who has lost his house to a fire and get him to share what it felt like to helplessly watch his house and cherished possessions go up in flames.

You could share statistics to show the likelihood that you may lose your house to a fire.

You could show an example of how quickly something as innocent looking as a candle could ignite a window curtain and thus the rest of the room.

Watching a video of this kind of event would be very powerful and would motivate people to buy the solution to this situation—a fire extinguisher.

And then you could literally demonstrate a completely different outcome with the same candle igniting the same curtains, but this time the homeowner is prepared and douses the flames in seconds with her fire extinguisher.

By tapping into the fear of loss, you would sell more fire extinguishers.

FEAR OF LOSS

The most common fear is the fear of loss when it comes to marketing. Whether it's the fear of losing money, a loved one, a house, a car, your health, or some other possession, fear of loss is the fear you'll use most often in marketing.

We've been well conditioned to feel fear. We see stories in the news all the time about people who have lost something. Maybe a house was swept away by a flood, or maybe parents lost a young child to some horrible disease. Whatever it was they lost, you could see (and feel) their pain by the look on their faces.

You work hard to have the things you have and to think it could all be swept away in a heartbeat can be very scary.

How about your health? How scary would it be to walk out of your doctor's office after being told you had cancer? Would your entire life flash before your eyes? Would your heart beat a little faster?

I could go on and on about the fears that people have. The key to this is to understand the fear that your product or service alleviates in the people who buy it, then tap into that fear in as many ways as you can.

A great place to do your research is the media. What are the biggest fears of the day? Is it the threat from terrorism, global warming, pollution, high taxes, divorce rates, cancer, attention-deficit/hyperactivity disorder, or any number of other things?

❧ SUCCESS STRATEGY ❧

Pay attention to the big news stories of the day. You can effectively tie the news to something your product or service does to protect people from having these things happen in their lives. If there is a story in the news about a family who just lost everything in a big fire, and you sell fire prevention equipment, use that story with a headline that reads, "Don't let this happen to you."

Once you have gathered this information from the media, step back and see if you can tie in a direct or an indirect benefit from your product or service to alleviate the fear. For example, if you offer a business opportunity, you could use the fear of high taxes to your benefit. Here's how.

In your marketing materials, you could focus on the fact that owning your own business is the perfect way to lower your tax bill, legally. In your presentation, you'd go on to explain how higher taxes will not affect you if you own a business and how higher taxes really only apply to people who work for somebody else.

Obviously, this is only one benefit of being in business for yourself, but it's a fear that is shared by many and highlighted in the media; it's a great idea to leverage this kind of fear in your marketing immediately.

Another fear shared by many people is that of falling sick. Think about the plethora of companies that sell vitamins, supplements, and herbal remedies. Although these companies can't usually make direct claims of curing a particular disease, they are not limited in how they use their client testimonials.

They may ask several thousand current customers to share their stories of success, and they will pull a small handful of the very best testimonials to use in their marketing. They can then target specific markets that may share a fear of a particular ailment, such as osteoporosis.

You could target your marketing to the groups who are most at risk for osteoporosis. Then you'd use the fear of getting this disease to motivate your prospects to take action and buy your remedy.

This may sound very simple, very logical, yet as I look at marketing materials that arrive in my e-mail inbox or my house mailbox day after day, I do not see this logical approach to emotional marketing, but rather a haphazard approach that rarely results in success.

Look at your marketing materials. Look at what you're selling. Can you find indirect benefits that alleviate a fear or fears shared by the majority of your market?

People in your market do have fears. Some people think this theory only applies to other people's markets, but it applies to your market as well. The challenge is to find those fears and then look at ways your product or service alleviates them.

REMOVING FEAR

In more than 23 years of consulting with clients in the area of marketing, I've never worked with a single client who could not find at least half a dozen reasons to include a fear element in his or her marketing materials.

Think about using deadlines and explaining what will happen if your prospect does not buy before a certain time or while supplies last.

Successful products provide solutions to problems or fears people face. This book is a great example. You likely picked up this book because you have an issue with your marketing or your sales. Rarely will a person pick up a book on marketing that does not address some sort of marketing challenge they would like to solve.

To sell you this book, I could have showed you how fast a business goes out of business if it doesn't fix its marketing problems immediately. How does it feel when you think your business could close its doors forever if you don't find ways to fix your marketing and do them right now?

Are you more motivated to buy and, even more important, read this book cover to cover? This is the power of using fear as an emotional motivator.

In the next chapter, we look at the second of five emotional motivators and how to use it in your marketing. Remember, if you decide not to continue reading now, you risk missing some of the most powerful marketing tools ever discovered.

If you don't have access to what I'm about to share with you, your business is at risk of not having marketing that works. And if you invest enough money in marketing that does not result in an increase in sales, you could be at risk of going bankrupt.

Where would you be without your business? What would you do? Who would get hurt if your business were to close its doors forever? Can you feel that empty feeling in your gut right now? Good. Maybe you've been made to feel the fear of not reading the rest of this book.

SAMPLE KEYWORDS AND PHRASES TO USE

- Don't miss out.
- Don't be left out.
- Only a limited number will be sold.
- Protect.

- Secure.
- Ends soon.
- Won't last.
- Supplies limited.
- Only 24 hours to take advantage.
- Just 10 people will be accepted.
- Missing out could cost you.

Are you ready for the next emotional motivator? Read on, my friend!

Emotional Motivator 2— Love

In this chapter, we shift away from fear and into what many people would consider as the opposite of fear—love. Before we get started, a little background is in order.

When I was in college, back in 1981, I remember creating a slide show about what is today known as the integration of technology. At the time, home computers were limited to two or three choices, and television had only 25 to 30 channels.

During my presentation, I drew a television in the center of the blackboard and then reasoned that with future technology, we'd be able to do most anything on our television. The mistake I made back then was to think that the television would still be the dominant technology. We know today that it is instead our computer. My mistake was drawing a television screen instead of a computer screen on the blackboard.

With the advent of computers, an interesting dynamic came to light. While we have more ways to communicate than at any time in history, we remain an isolated society.

Your gut reaction might be to refute this, and I was with you at one time. With cell phones, pagers, e-mail, faxes, instant messaging, text messaging, couriers, mail, digital delivery, telephones, web sites, and more, you'd think we'd be a society that communicates.

The reverse is actually true. We see each other in person less and less. We speak even less and rely more and more on e-mail. We have learned how to hide behind our e-mail and do business that way instead of in person with a firm handshake.

The challenge with this is that we are wired biologically to connect with other human beings. While we can do most of what we need to on a single computer screen, our hearts long for human contact.

What happens to the person who is stuck behind a computer screen all day for months and months at a time? They get a lot done, but what they miss is human contact. This is a powerful motivator and one worth looking into.

People need to connect with others, and the way things are set up today for most people, connecting happens only through electronic means, which isn't quite good enough. You now know of an emotional motivator that can get people to take action. Let's look how connection works in the marketing world.

LOVE AS A MOTIVATOR

If you love marketing, you likely share my passion for observing what happens in the business world. It's certainly the best place to learn what works and what's nothing more than hype. Observation is where the bulk of my early marketing education came from, and I've never stopped looking at what goes on because things are constantly changing. There is no stopping the learning process when it comes to marketing, no matter how long you remain in the field.

The emotional motivator called *love* is actually broken down into three levels: (1) connection, (2) love, and (3) sex. As in life, there are many flavors of love, so it is in the marketing world.

I'm not going to get into a big philosophical discussion about *love* and what it means, what it could mean, or what it really means. The word love has hundreds of definitions, but for the purpose of marketing, they are not overly important.

It is important, however, to realize that people have an innate desire to love and be loved. Although we've created a society that can exist in principle with minimal human contact, it falls short of being truly fulfilling.

Think about that the next time you pull up to an automated teller machine (ATM) instead of walking into the bank and speaking with a live teller. Does it make a difference to you? Do you even notice?

Chances are you don't notice because it's been many years since banks relied on a teller for each transaction. This is just one example of how our society now relies more on computers and machines and less on human interaction.

Need I remind you of the computer you use to gain access to the Internet? How many fewer phone calls do you make now that you can instant message or e-mail somebody instead? How many fewer handwritten cards do you send in favor of a quick e-mail?

The picture is easy to see. We're becoming more and more disassociated with other people. The next generation is growing up with electronic babysitters (e.g., videos, computer games, DVDs) and becoming even more disassociated than my generation.

The net effect of this is that our craving for love is as high as it's ever been. We want to connect with others as often as possible, but more and more we connect via electronic means instead.

CONNECTION

Connection is the lowest level of the love emotional motivator and doesn't require any romantic involvement. It's a conversation, a look into another person's eyes, a handshake, or simply belonging to a social group.

When you look at the business world, can you find examples of businesses selling using connection as a motivational motivator? This one is in fact quite common and it won't take you more than a few moments to think of a business using connection to sell their products and services.

Over the past few years, a new breed of web site has appeared in the online world with an unheard of force. The broad category is known as *social networking*. These sites open and start with just a few users and soon blossom into millions and tens of millions of subscribers.

What do you think is going on here? Could it have anything to do with that big, unfulfilled need to connect with other human beings?

❦ SUCCESS STRATEGY ❦

No matter what kind of event, product, or service you offer, look for ways you can add the element of networking to your offering. In a live event, networking is a natural part of the program; make sure it's prominently displayed in your marketing pieces. If you offer a hard product, you may provide free access to a web site for users to network with one another and share tips, techniques, stories, and more.

Where are people going to socialize these days? Many are turning on their computers and trying to replicate human interaction online.

In my own business, I've often used connection to promote my live seminars. The way to do this is to use two key words in your marketing copy. Those words are "join us."

These two words imply that by coming to this seminar you'll be joining a group of like-minded people who are looking for answers to the same questions as you.

People jump at the chance to connect with others and when you can offer them the opportunity to join your group, you are indeed hitting the emotional love button at the level of connection.

This is why membership businesses work, networking groups have become so popular, and so many social networking web sites have exploded onto the scene in recent years.

LOVE: THE ULTIMATE EMOTION

Moving up from connection, the next motivational level is *love*. Love in this way means that people are looking for long-term relationships or marriage. Romantic love is the kind of love I'm speaking about.

Can you think of businesses that sell romantic love? This one is really simple. Dating services first appeared online in the mid-1980s. Yes, there was an online world back then, but there were only a couple of dating services. After the debut of the World Wide Web in 1992, these services moved to the Internet and soon after began to explode in popularity.

These sites differ greatly from the social networking sites in that the aim of the sites is to play matchmaker and help you to find your soul mate. As we have become more and more isolated, these types of businesses continue to blossom.

Dating web sites represent one of the fastest-growing business categories on the Internet and have been so for more than a decade. Dating sites often begin quietly and then explode with hundreds of thousands of users in just months.

Some of the bigger dating web sites boast as many as 25 million active subscribers. These are all people who are primarily seeking love because it's an emotion that is missing in their lives and it's an emotion they truly want to feel.

Think of Match.com or eHarmony.com as two of the largest and most successful online dating services.

The emotion of love is used by all kinds of businesses. Think about those ads for sports cars you've seen all your life. Picture an ordinary-looking man stepping into a hot new candy-apple-red turbo ZX445. The ad then shows a beautiful woman's head turning as this man drives the car past her.

Not all commercials for cars are like this, but the general idea is the same. The car becomes the vehicle to love. Get the car; get the girl. It also works in reverse when the car company targets their ads to women. This time it's the beautiful woman in the car, and it's the man whose head is turning.

Love is used in other ads targeted to women. You may see an ad with a photo of a beautiful woman all dressed up and holding that bottle of the perfect scent. Over her shoulder, a little off in the distance and looking right at her is the perfect man, dressed in a tuxedo and looking perfect in every way.

What's being sold here? The implication is that the perfume will attract the perfect man. The perfume is in the ad, but it hardly matters because it's the relationship, or potential relationship, between the man and the woman that is making the sale.

To see many more examples of these kinds of ads, many with few or even no words in the ad, pick up a copy of *Vogue* magazine the next time you stop by the bookstore. Love is the primary emotional motivator used in many of the ads you'll see in *Vogue* and other similar magazines targeted to women.

Love is a powerful emotional motivator and as such requires a lot less convincing to get a prospect to buy into it because people are already actively looking to fulfill their desire for love in their lives.

SEX: THE NEXT LEVEL

What happens when love rises to the next level? The marketing process begins with connection, moving to love and then to the higher level of sex. Yes, we're going to speak about sex; well, from a marketing perspective anyway.

You've heard it said many times, "Sex sells." It does. And if you can find ways to incorporate sex into your advertising, sales will go up.

I was browsing some ads on eBay the other day and I found it very interesting that one fellow was using a photo of a pretty woman in his ad. Now you might not find this too unusual unless you knew what he was selling.

This person was selling speakers. What did the photo of the pretty woman have to do with these speakers? Absolutely nothing, but when I checked to see how many people had viewed his ads, the numbers spoke for themselves.

His ad was viewed more than five times the number of the other ads. The picture, by the way, was of a woman in a skimpy bathing suit. The issue was that while he was attracting many viewers, he missed connecting the picture of the woman to his speakers, so his viewers left without placing a bid!

Had he been more in tune with using sex to sell in his ad, he may have had the woman in the skimpy bathing suit holding the speakers, or maybe lying out in the sun listening to her favorite music on his speakers.

It's not that you're actually selling connection, love, or sex in your ads. It's that you're making the connection between your product or service and the emotion generated by the thought of sex.

Many of the ads you'll see on a daily basis use sex to sell their wares, but it's not always overt. The model in the ads does have her clothes on, but the look on her face or the way she is posed tells the viewer that sex is possible.

Let's go back to our example of the diet pills. Could you sell the diet pills with sex? Of course you can, and many companies do.

To make this work, all you'd need is a photo of a perfectly thin woman in a sexy outfit or swimsuit holding your bottle of pills. The viewer will put the pieces together and will be motivated by the emotions of love and sex to purchase those pills.

If you were trying to appeal to a mixed audience of men and women, just add a great-looking man to the photo and make sure there is some form of flirty connection happening between the two. Now you have an ad that will appeal to both men and women by implying love and sex at the same time.

Obviously, this does not work on every person who will ever view that ad, but it will reach a large portion of your target market. Later in this book, we see how to combine all five emotional motivators in a single ad to reach more viewers.

❧ SUCCESS STRATEGY ❧

Use photos whenever possible for communicating the message of connection/love/sex. A single photograph can do more for your marketing piece than a page full of words.

Selling sex on the Internet is big business. It was the most profitable business category of the entire Internet during its first decade of existence. It remains extremely profitable to this day and it's easy to understand why.

Less human contact combined with the same level of desire for love and sex reveals why this particular emotional motivator is so incredibly powerful. People buy products and services they feel will lead them to sex.

Whether it's the latest perfume, the hottest sports car, the most luxurious cruise vacation, or even the latest computer system, people will buy it if they truly feel it will lead to sex.

I know it sounds horrible to think of your market in this way, but the numbers for many generations have proven that people do many things they would not otherwise do if they feel it will lead to sex.

The overriding emotion far outweighs any level of logic. If the emotional want is for sex and you have found a way to use an indirect benefit to show how your product or service could lead to sex, you'll dramatically increase your sales.

It also crosses all age barriers. Studies show that people in their 70s, 80s, and even 90s are still motivated by sex. It's not age dependant.

Stop by your local bookstore and have a look at the periodicals section. Look for the magazines that use sex on the front cover to sell the magazine. I've always been fascinated by looking at the covers of car and motorcycle magazines. Inevitably, there is a scantily clad woman draped over the hood of the car or over the handlebars of a motorcycle. These women have nothing to do with the content of the publication, but sex sells. If you can associate sex with your product or service, people will buy it more often. So the women on these covers hint at sex and the person looking at the car then associates sex with the car on the cover, and more important, with the magazine, which then becomes a must-have item for them so they buy a copy of the magazine.

The publisher is happy because they sell more magazines, attract more subscriptions, and can then charge more for advertising. The reader is happy, at least in the moment, because they have the feeling that a primary human emotional want is being fulfilled. And the customer may not even be consciously aware of why he is attracted to the magazine, he only knows he wants a copy and wants it now!

Since you can't actually sell sex in a magazine, you sell the feeling of attracting sex by using the product, reading the magazine, or buying the car.

The key to understanding how this works is that you don't necessarily need to be selling sex to make this a powerful marketing tool. Remember, sex triggers emotion and all you really need to do is hint at sex to make this emotional motivator work for you.

Clients of mine have added a picture of a pretty woman holding their product on their home page. Why would you do such a thing? What benefit could you possibly gain by having a picture of a pretty woman holding your product?

The answer is that it does get people to stop and spend some time on your web site when they would otherwise just click away a few seconds after the site loads. This is especially true if your market is primarily comprised of male prospects.

However, studies have shown that even women will stop and look, more out of curiosity, when there is a pretty woman in the picture. When asked why a woman would be attracted by the image of another woman, most responded with answers having to do with being curious about what it was about that woman that gets a man's attention.

If you're wondering if this really works, just walk by a magazine rack. What you'll find is magazine covers with pretty women on them. This is true not just of male-focused publications but also of publications that target women. Think of *Cosmo* magazine. You'll rarely see an issue with anything but a female model on the front cover and *Cosmo* is a decidedly female-focused magazine.

The reasoning behind this approach is obvious. It's instructive to look at it closer to find new ways to use this emotional motivator in your own marketing materials.

If you're struggling with trying to figure out how to use connection, love, and sex in your marketing, don't worry. You're going to see some examples later on in this book. As we continue, you're sure to find dozens of ways to use this emotional motivator in your business, regardless of what you sell.

SAMPLE KEYWORDS AND PHRASES TO USE

- Join us.
- Network with others.
- Meet people just like you.
- Be a part of.
- Connection.
- Meet your soul mate.
- Relationship.
- Intimate.
- Seductive.
- Sensual.
- Sexy.

Now, let's look at number three of the five emotional motivators.

CHAPTER 6

Emotional Motivator 3— Freebies and Bargains

The third emotional motivator is broken into two categories: (1) getting something for free and (2) getting a bargain. Although they are similar, they are best covered separately. Let's start with getting something free.

FREEBIES: GETTING SOMETHING FOR FREE

One of the most powerful words in the language of marketing has to be the word *free*. Anytime we see this word, we stop, take notice, and ask ourselves questions such as:

- ✔ What's free?
- ✔ Where can I get it?
- ✔ Can I get more than one?

One of the best parts of using the word *free* in your marketing is that no matter what you sell, regardless of the market in which you sell, you can always include something free in your offers.

Not once have I worked with any business where I could not integrate something free in their advertising. This doesn't mean you have to give away the store just to make a sale. The free item you offer could be something that actually costs you nothing to produce or duplicate such as an e-book or an audio download.

There is always a way to tack on a free item to a purchase, and one great strategy is to have that free item be provided by somebody else. As an example of this, look to the airline industry. When you get your boarding pass, they give you a free paper jacket to make it convenient for you to carry your boarding pass (or passes) with you.

That paper jacket is *not* paid for by the airline although their name and logo appear all over it. There is another company that provides these paper jackets to the airlines at no cost. The genius in this process is that the company that provides the paper jackets uses other people's money to pay for them.

Who gets the bill for the millions of paper jackets that are distributed every year? The other companies who pay to advertise on these paper jackets pay for it all. The money raised by selling advertising on these paper jackets is used to cover the cost of printing them. The leftover money, which runs into millions of dollars each year, is the profit the company keeps for putting this all together.

They can easily provide these paper jackets to the airlines and not charge them a penny for them. The next time you're on an airplane, pull out that paper jacket and have a look at who's really paying for it.

A simpler example is one that I often use in my own business. I create audio programs that are available either as audio CDs or as digital downloads. I make these available to my clients as free gifts when they purchase other items from my company.

These audio downloads may be interviews I've conducted with other prominent figures in my market or training programs

I've created for my customers. They may actually be existing programs currently for sale on my web site. It all depends on what I'm using the free bonus for.

But it doesn't end there. I also make these audio downloads available to other companies to use as free bonus items. This way, anytime their customers make a purchase from them, my audio file is delivered to that customer as well. How it works for both of us is actually quite simple.

For every audio download they provide to their clients, the client ends up with a great bonus item they did not have to pay for, and I get the name and contact information of that client.

In this way, we both win. The other company gets a bonus item they can offer free to their customers, which increases their sales, and I get the name and contact information of their customer to add to my master database. The client also wins by getting a powerful, information-rich audio they can listen to over and over again.

There is also a longer-term win in this for me. As these clients listen to my audio download, they are introduced to me and my business. Now when I go back to them with an offer, they are much more likely to purchase from me since they have already had some exposure to my work.

It makes sense to provide these audio programs to as many companies as possible because it extends my reach in the marketplace, helps to build my prospect database, and results in more sales over time for my business.

HOW MANY PENS ARE ENOUGH?

Not too long ago, I was exhibiting at a trade show for small business and I had placed a pile of pens on my exhibiting table with my company name, web site, and phone number imprinted on the barrels of these pens.

All day long, people would stop by my booth, not because they really cared what I had to offer, but because they wanted the free pens. One man came by, grabbed an entire handful of my pens, and just walked away. He didn't even stop to say hello. He just grabbed the pens and walked off.

This man had on a suit and tie and was obviously in business, but the urge to get something for free motivated him to grab my pens. I might have done better to hand them out rather than have them on my table for anybody to grab, but it did bring people to my booth.

People are indeed driven to take action by things they can get for free. You could give away free e-books, special reports, white papers, guides, manuals, audio downloads, and more to attract people to your web site. This is indeed how most Internet businesses today build their lists.

Even if you're not marketing on the Internet, you can still use information products as freebies. In many cases, sending out an audio CD is much better than offering people a link to an MP3 download. The CD holds much more value in your client's mind than does a download, which they know costs you nothing.

In every business I work with, I'll do everything I can to at the very least capture the contact information of the people requesting the free offer. This way, even if they don't make a purchase today, I have their information and can market to them again in a few days.

You must be smart about what it is you're giving away. You could give away a free vacation in Hawaii and get thousands of people to come to your web site and sign up for their chance to win. The problem is that you'd end up with a list of people who want a free vacation and probably have no interest in what you're really trying to sell them.

This is a common, easy-to-make mistake. Yes, people do respond to things they can get for free, but you have to set up some rules around the free giveaway to make it work for your business.

A better approach would be to correctly, and directly, align the free offer with the product or service you're selling. A carpet cleaner may offer to clean your couch free when they clean your entire home's carpets. This aligns with the offer and makes perfect sense. This kind of offer will lead to an increase in business, with minimal cost to the business owner.

A chiropractor might offer to do an additional examination procedure not normally covered during a normal office visit for an adjustment. This will bring in more patients, and the only cost is the additional time required for the free service.

An Internet marketer might include several free bonus items, all digitally delivered, to increase the number of sales generated on the web. Another offer might be for a free audio CD or DVD, which has a duplication cost that can be measured in pennies, yet adds great value to the core product or service.

HIGH PERCEIVED VALUE

Offering a free item to increase the response to your advertising or to increase sales is contingent on the item that is offered having a high perceived value in the eyes of your customer or prospect.

You're not going to get anybody to respond to an offer that includes something free that they can get anywhere, or that is of no value to them. Yet, in my everyday experiences, I see these offers all the time.

The most common offenders are Internet marketers who give away free reports that can be years old with outdated information and that can no longer be sold. Retail stores often do this by giving away inventory they couldn't otherwise sell. Please don't follow this example.

Sometimes, companies offer freebies of such little value that even though I buy an advertised product, I tell the company to keep the freebie. It's more of a hassle for me to take it and then trash it, so I just leave it behind and let them deal with it instead.

❧ SUCCESS STRATEGY ❧

Getting donations of items with a high-perceived value as bonuses can be as simple as asking for them. Show the owners of the potential bonus item how it would benefit their business to include their offering with your sales. Go one step further and offer to give them the contact information for each customer who gets their donated bonus item.

Many marketing companies offer items such as free alarm clock radios as gifts when you purchase from their catalog. This practice has been going on for years, and it makes sense in some markets to use this approach. Here's how it works.

The marketer will do some research online to find companies overseas that can provide the premium item they want to offer free to their customers. One great resource for that is www.Alibaba.com.

There are dozens of manufacturers who offer electronic products at prices so low it will make your head spin, so companies contract with the manufacturer to purchase a seagoing container of the product they have chosen.

They may find a manufacturer of clock radios and be able to purchase them in volume for as little as a dollar or two each. What makes this type of free offer work is that the perceived value of the clock radio may be as high as $50 to the client or prospect.

The rule of thumb here is simple. If you can't sell it, you won't be able to give it away. If what you're trying to use as a free giveaway has no value to your clients or prospects; it will not help you make more sales.

BARGAINS: WHAT'S ON SALE?

The second part of this emotional motivator is getting a bargain. A bargain is being able to buy the product or service for less than it is valued. Think about this in terms of offering a sale, or offering the wholesale pricing that companies such as Costco and Sam's Club offer every day.

This is why there is always a long wait to check out of these giant warehouse stores and why there is a trend toward even larger big-box stores that offer lower than retail pricing.

Today, we are much more savvy shoppers. We have many tools at our fingertips that allow us to shop for the best price on an item once we've decided what item we want to purchase.

The trend is to now cater to the savvy shoppers by making it easy for them to find the best price on something. Wal-Mart was founded on this premise. Offer customers the lowest price, guaranteed.

Is Wal-Mart successful? Are there lines at any Wal-Mart store, even at 10:00 P.M.? What do you think is really going on here? Could it be that people really are motivated by crowded department stores? Could it be that people have nothing better to do with their time than bump-and-weave their way down all-too-narrow aisles for hours?

Or could it be that the emotional motivator of saving a few dollars, backed up by a price guarantee, motivates this behavior. There are other examples in the marketplace.

Home Depot is yet another big-box store that attracts crowds week after week, day after day. What's the main driving force here? Could it be that getting tools and building supplies at lower than retail pricing is what created this giant company?

How about Costco or Sam's Club? These two huge successes are yet again based on the idea of getting valuable products at a bargain. This is a powerful emotional motivator that is well worth exploring in your own business.

I know you've heard of www.eBay.com, right? What do you think made this business grow like a wind-driven California wildfire? Think about it. Every product offered on eBay is offered at prices usually well below retail. It is a bargain hunter's paradise. There are many business owners who have equipped their offices with all the latest and greatest technology, all purchased for a reduced price on eBay.

If you don't shop eBay all that often, it would be a great idea for you to visit the web site and start looking for some of the things you would normally buy just to see how much of a bargain you can get on eBay instead.

As a youngster, I remember how busy a particular retail store would be anytime they ran their "One Day Sale" events. I'd be dragged to this store as a child, but only on these sale days.

Parking was always a challenge. The store was jammed with people, and finding your size in anything was a crapshoot at best. By the end of the day, the store looked like it had been host to a riot.

Inventory was low, and the store was a wreck. However, the store's bank account was full, and the store's management was very pleased.

On the days when there was no such sale, the store was clean, parking was easy, and inventory was plentiful. But prices were regular prices and not sale prices. There were always some customers in the store, but the numbers were next to nothing when compared to sale days.

The emotional motivator of getting a bargain works best when there is an established relationship with your clients or prospects and they also know the regular prices you charge for your products and services.

For a retail store, the people who show up for the sales are the same people who shop there on the nonsale days as well. They know what's offered, and they have a good idea of how much things cost.

They also know the store offers a certain quality of product with which they are comfortable and when the store lowers its prices for a sale, these very same people are the ones who will show up for the sale.

An example of how this emotional motivator does not work well is in the case of the person selling a product that nobody is familiar with. Maybe you've created an informational program and now you've priced it at $97.

But you have not done any real marketing and have not made the point clearly enough that this program is truly valued at $97. If you go out and try to sell this same program at a discount on eBay, for example, it may be puzzling to you when you do not make any sales.

You're insulted that people would not buy your $97 program for even $1 on eBay. How could that be?

You have to first establish a base price in the minds of your customers and prospects so they are aware of the value of your program. You might do this with your list of customers and prospects as you market your program to them over and over again at your $97 price point.

After they have seen you offer the program at $97 for some time, they will get the idea that your program is indeed worth $97.

If, one day, you decide to offer this same program to these same people, but today, you offer it at $49 instead of $97, the chances are very high that you'll sell many more of these products at the new discounted price.

The retail store that does not ever offer their products at regular price will benefit little by offering them on sale. This is why you don't see Wal-Mart holding "one-day" sales. They sell at the lowest price, everyday.

There is a trap in selling only on price. Once you train your customers to the fact that you'll hold a sale every four weeks, for example, you'll all but stop making sales at your regular prices. Your client will wait to buy from you on your sales days and that's it.

There is a woman who owns a little bookstore locally who offers readings with a psychic. The normal routine for her is to offer all psychic readings for half-price once a month on the third Saturday of the month.

What happens is that the regular customers plan to come on the sales days to get their readings done at half price, but they don't come when regular prices are in effect.

A better approach might be to hold your sales at unpredictable intervals so that your customers do not sit back and wait for your next sale on the third Saturday of the month.

This is the proper way to use the emotional motivator of getting something for a bargain in your business.

There has to be an established value to a product or service offering either by your company, or by other companies. If I'm going to sell a popular electronics item on eBay at a bargain price, it will sell because the market already knows what the true value of this product is.

So it's not just your efforts that establish the value, it's also the people in your market who may be offering the same, or greatly similar, product or service. Once the value is established in your marketplace, you can then effectively use this emotional motivator to increase your sales.

We are—by nature, it seems—programmed to look for and find bargains on just about everything. Whether it's a new house, new furniture, a new car, a home mortgage, or a gallon of milk, we're trained to look for the best price we can get.

There's nothing wrong with looking for a great price on the things we buy. It's really what makes our economy work as well as it does. The key, as a marketer, is to realize that your market is always looking for a bargain and it's your job to find ways to bring those bargains to them.

USING FREEBIES AND BARGAINS

The emotional motivator of getting a freebie or a bargain has something for every business. In later chapters, you find further examples of how to use these two powerful motivators in all your advertising and marketing materials.

People respond to free offers and they respond to sales and bargains. Think about what you offer and find as many ways to incorporate either or both of these motivators in your marketing. You'll immediately benefit with increased traffic to your business and increased sales volume, too.

SAMPLE KEYWORDS AND PHRASES TO USE

- Free.
- Free offer.
- Free trial.
- Free bonus.
- No cost.
- Half price.
- Save.
- Sale.
- Prices slashed.
- 24-hour sale.

Next up, the emotional motivator used most often in the business world.

CHAPTER 7

Emotional Motivator 4— Effortless Moneymaking

T his emotional motivator is one of the more popular ones, yet at first glance, effortless moneymaking doesn't appear to apply to every business. Let's see how I've been able to apply this next emotional motivator to almost every business using indirect benefits, sometimes very creatively.

The emotional motivator of effortless moneymaking is what drives the get-rich-quick industry. You should pay close attention to not just the "moneymaking" part of this emotional motivator, but to the word "effortless." Using no effort is the key to this emotional motivator, and that is why this emotional motivator works so incredibly well.

We have become a "push-button" society in many respects. When we want to know something, we point and click and there's our answer.

If we're hungry, dial a few numbers, tell the voice on the other end what we want, and they bring it to us. If we're not happy with what we see on television, push a few buttons and we can watch something else.

The Internet age has indeed made us a push-button society and that has raised the bar of expectations to all new levels. We're no longer willing to sit behind the same desk doing the same work for a meager 3 percent raise every year.

Instead, if we're not happy doing the work we're doing, we go on the Internet, post our resume, and within hours, we have new opportunities to review. We want results, and we're no longer willing to wait.

This trend will continue because technology has such a profound effect on our lives. It is well worth your time to figure out ways to make your business deliver quick results.

One industry that really amazes me these days is the mortgage industry. As a kid, I remember that it would take months to go through the process of buying a new home. It took weeks of not knowing anything to find out if your mortgage would be approved.

Today, when you apply, you get an answer back the same day. The waiting game is over and it's just another sign that everything in our lives is moving much faster.

Armed with this knowledge, you can now begin to see why effortless moneymaking is such a powerful concept. Imagine the person who is sitting at home staring at a pile of bills from all those too-easy-to-get credit cards and who has no way of paying more than the minimum payment each month.

What do you think is on this person's mind at this moment?

Could he be wondering how these bills are going to be paid?

Do you think he wants a simple, fast solution, or is he expecting to pay the bills over the next decade or more?

The way we've been trained to think is in terms of finding the quickest, easiest solution to the current problem. If you doubt this statement, just turn on your television any night of the week and watch a few 30-minute infomercials.

These programs are all about solving a problem quickly and easily, and they rake in millions and millions of dollars each day. That's why they are on the air and stay on the air, often for years on end. Think about it.

One of the biggest challenges we want solved is the issue of not having enough money. Lack of money is by far the biggest of all challenges faced by most people in our society today. This is why effortless moneymaking is such a powerful emotional motivator.

❧ SUCCESS STRATEGY ❧

Whenever you can clearly show your prospects how much money they can make with your product or service, you can easily raise your prices above your competitors. Consider this idea: "Would you pay me $100,000 to consult with you if I were to bring in an additional $1 million in sales for your company?" This is an incredible deal that represents just 10 percent of the increase in income your company would receive. However, if my offer were positioned as a flat $100,000 consulting fee, it would appear astronomically expensive. It's the promise of income from the consulting that brings the high price into a new perspective.

Let's look at where effortless moneymaking shows up in our society to get an idea of the size and scope of the power of this emotional motivator.

Recently, I spoke about effortless moneymaking in Las Vegas at Caesar's Palace. The group had come to participate in a weekend seminar I hosted on Internet marketing. As I began my presentation on this particular emotional motivator, effortless moneymaking, I asked the group if they had seen any examples of effortless moneymaking on their way up to the seminar room.

There was that long pause in the room as I waited for an answer, any answer. No answer came, so I walked to the center of the room and pretended I was pulling a quarter from my pocket and slipping it into a slot, then pulling a handle. I then stepped back and waited to see the results of my actions.

I then pretended that I'd won the jackpot and jumped up and down repeatedly. They got the point.

Is it effortless to slip a quarter into a machine? You bet it is. How about pulling that handle? Well, for some older folks it might not be effortless, but the casinos have fixed that. All the player has to do now is push a button.

Is it effortless to sit back and wait to see if you won the jackpot? You bet it is.

What's really going on here is that you've been presented with an effortless way to make, what could possibly be, thousands of dollars with a quarter and the push of a button or the pull of a lever.

This promise of effortless moneymaking takes in hundreds of millions of dollars each day in the United States. And there is no end in sight.

People want easy (effortless) ways to become rich and they have good reason to expect it to happen, too. Just look around at all the casinos that have popped up in the past decade. This trend will continue, but it's not the only one.

PLAY THE LOTTERY

What about the lottery? Is it relatively effortless? Is there a promise of big money behind it? You bet! (Pun intended.) For just $1, you stand the chance of winning millions of dollars.

Isn't that why the lottery is so popular? Isn't that why it's such a moneymaker for the governments who run and control these programs?

The lure is so strong that I've met many corporate CEOs who already make millions of dollars but who still buy lottery tickets every week. Could this emotional motivator really be powerful enough that it crosses all social and economic boundaries? I've seen evidence that it does at many seminars where I've spoken. Doctors, lawyers, accountants, fire fighters, police officers, military, you name it, they come to these events looking for effortless ways to bring in more money.

In my regular business, I make sure to have this emotional motivator covered because I know that people who are seeking marketing advice are, in reality, looking for effortless ways to make more money in their businesses.

Marketing is the best way to bring in more money to your business, and done properly it can be effortless. If you think about the premise for this book, motivational marketing, it's about effortlessly making more money by tapping into the emotional reasons people make a buying decision.

Business owners who already invest in marketing can make a few small changes to existing ads and double, triple, or even quadruple the size of their business in a very short period of time.

That's exciting. It's effortless. And it works. Do you want to know more about it? Keep reading.

GET RICH QUICK

Where else does this concept of effortless moneymaking show up in our society? Have you ever picked up a magazine that promotes home businesses? The industry we know as the get-rich-quick industry began decades ago as the mail-order business.

You may remember the early programs where you'd stay at home and stuff envelopes and some company would pay you money for every envelope you stuffed. Then in the 1970s, the world of network marketing or multilevel marketing began to emerge.

To this day, this industry remains very active. It would be a great exercise to skim through the ads in any home business magazine just to see how hard they push the effortless money-making emotional button in their advertising.

When I first began my marketing career, this is exactly what I did. I'd look over these ads and ask why I was attracted to them? What was I really looking to get from them? I wanted to know which emotional button had been pushed that made me call a toll-free number at 2:00 A.M.

That was really powerful and I knew I wasn't the only person making those late-night calls since the ads usually said call any time. I remember sitting in bed one night and I decided to do a little more research on the subject, so I called, one after another, just about every ad I could find with a phone number in the classified ads section of a home business magazine.

Within days, my mailbox was jammed with get-rich-quick programs, tapes, seminar invitations, offers to join membership programs, and much more. My phone rang off the hook with people trying hard to sell me into their programs. It was a great lesson.

At that time, money was hard to come by. I was working in marketing, but had not reached a level of income that matched my level of expenses. (You've heard that story before, I'm sure.)

I wanted and needed more money, yet I loved what I was doing and had little extra time to pursue anything else. Despite that, these ads spoke to me, loud and clear.

"Make Money Stuffing Envelopes," one headline read and I thought, "I could do that while I'm watching television."

"Make One Sale, Get Paid for Life." Another headline shouted. I thought, "I could do that."

These headlines are clearly targeted to my emotional desire for more money without much effort invested. And they work.

Here's what's even more interesting. To this day, I still read those ads. Money is no longer an issue in my life, but the allure of the ads is almost addicting. While I no longer respond to these ads, I do look at them to borrow ideas for headlines for my own advertising.

I pay particular attention to ads that run in the same magazine month after month. They are the winners. No marketer in the world is going to invest his money in an ad that does not produce results, so I look for the ads that run repeatedly, and I feel pretty confident these ads work.

There is no better way to learn than to look at what's already working. This is how I started, and it's how I show people who are interested in marketing how to get started. It's a habit you may well want to acquire as well.

Effortless moneymaking doesn't end with advertising. When you attend a seminar in most industries, you're likely to run into a presenter who uses the emotional motivator of effortless moneymaking as part of his or her sales pitch.

I've seen it at dental conferences, insurance expos, colleges, and even churches. This particular emotional motivator is far-reaching because money is the one thing that just about everybody struggles with.

It's interesting to track the latest moneymaking trends in this country. You can find these by watching the seminar circuit and seeing what's taught at those events.

For the longest time, real estate was all the rage. There were seminars everywhere telling people how they could buy real estate with none of their own money and turn that into tens of thousands of dollars in profit, usually in under a year.

Then the real estate market sagged and the seminars stopped drawing crowds. Not to put an end to a good thing, the next rage became investing in the stock market. There were all kinds of seminars on the topic of how to trade your way to wealth sitting at home in your underwear.

Then it was the Internet. You could set up a simple web site and become a millionaire even if you didn't know how to turn on your computer. When that trend died down, it went back to real estate. Then back to the stock market. You get the idea.

There always has been, and will likely always be, a get-rich-quick game that attracts the masses and generates millions and millions of dollars in profit for its promoters.

It's not my place to say if these programs work or not because I've not purchased and tried them all. I can say, however, that the many I've tried did not work as promised. If you're going to get involved, ask to speak to people who are already involved and find out how it's working for them.

CREATING EFFORTLESS MONEYMAKING

There are a number of ways to promote your offering using the emotional motivator of effortless moneymaking. First, if what you sell will help somebody bring in extra money, you will be able to use this emotional motivator as a direct benefit.

If your product or service offering is some sort of business opportunity, motivating this way is not going to be very difficult for you. But the chances are that what you're offering may not be a business opportunity or even a money-making opportunity.

If that's the case, then you have to think outside the box to find ways in which to fit effortless moneymaking into your marketing. After all, most people want extra money, so it makes sense to work hard to fit this emotional motivator into your marketing.

You might do this by explaining how the use of the products or services your company provides might save your customers money.

If you were selling car insurance, you might start with the fact that your rates are cheaper than the competition's rates on the same policy. Then you might play with the suggestion of "What will you do with the extra money you'll save when you work with us?"

The idea is to illustrate that saving money is the same as making money, and the money you save can help you buy and do the things you want.

Saving money is effortless. If I come into your store to get my clothes dry-cleaned and, instead of being charged the normal prices, I get a 30 percent discount, then I just saved that money. It took no effort. I didn't have to say anything, do anything, or jump through any hoops. I just did what I normally do, and now I'm paying less for the same service. I've got extra money in my pocket that can be used however I want.

While this can be similar to getting something for a bargain price, or on sale, it will differ in how you present the offer to your customers. Either way is powerful in motivating people to buy from you.

It's up to you to find as many ways as possible to illustrate that saving money by buying from you is a benefit in the same emotional way as making money.

Does this mean you go out and put everything on sale? No.

Instead, you can clearly illustrate to your prospects that buying from you might mean fewer maintenance costs, or that your product will last twice as long as the competition's product.

When I went to look for a new car, I stopped by the local BMW dealership. The car's price is higher than most American-made brands, so they had to work hard to get me to fork over the additional money for their cars.

Their approach was simple. The dealer asked me how much I had spent on maintenance for my American-made car in the past five years. When I thought about it, the car was in the shop every three months, on average, and I'd spent thousands in repairs. The brakes went every 15,000 miles. Then it was the muffler. Then it was the transmission. It seemed the expenses never ended.

When I added it up in my head, I could see that while the purchase price was lower for the American-made cars, the maintenance made up for the difference.

When I looked at the higher price of the BMW, the dealer told me all I'd have to worry about for the next five years were wipers and tires—the rest was covered in the price of the car. I knew from the moment I drove that car off the lot how much it would cost me to maintain that new BMW over the next five years.

The dealer used their guarantee to show me how easy it would be to own a BMW because all the maintenance was included in the price. I knew I'd buy the car because of the time I would save not waiting to have my car serviced every three months. Instead, I could come in every six to nine months and they would give me a loaner car. I'd be in and out of the dealership in 15 minutes.

That was effortless money to me. I was sold when I realized that I would not lose time waiting around to be told my car needed thousands of dollars in repairs. I was so sold that I may not ever consider buying any other brand of car!

What if you sell a service such as chiropractic care? This is easy when you think outside the box. I could ask, "How much does it cost you every day that you're not feeling your absolute best?"

For many people, every day lost at work might mean hundreds of dollars in productivity. In this case, I would position my chiropractic care as the only health care service that actually makes you money by making sure you stay healthy day after day.

While it might seem like a stretch, when you speak to a chiropractor, you'll understand that what he does is really more preventative in nature than it is to fix a problem you may already have. Although he does both, the main benefit to regular chiropractic care is a reduced incidence of illness.

Any day I spend working on my business instead of being too sick to work is extra money in my pocket, so I buy chiropractic care.

Another example could be the diet pills I spoke about earlier in this book. How can they lead to effortless moneymaking? If you lose the weight, you'll have more energy and can do more at work. This increase in energy may lead to getting a promotion or a raise. That is effortless.

But there's more to this as well, and I cover it in great detail later in this book. For now, just remember to think outside the box and use those indirect benefits to show how your product or service can result in effortless moneymaking.

This is a powerful emotional motivator, so do all you can to incorporate it into your marketing materials.

SAMPLE KEYWORDS AND PHRASES TO USE

- Make money while you sleep.
- So easy, even a fifth grader could do it.
- Make one sale, get paid again and again.
- Effortless.
- You could win.
- Enter to win.
- Nothing to do.
- We do it all for you.
- Your computer does all the work.

Let's go on to the next emotional motivator.

CHAPTER

Emotional Motivator 5— Making Dreams Come True

This is the final emotional motivator, and we all share this hope in one way or another. Although this emotional motivator relates to "having your dreams come true," you could also call it "reaching your goals."

I prefer to see this one as having dreams come true primarily because not everybody actually sets goals. While goal setting is taught in almost every success seminar, in reality, it's practiced by very few people. However, we all have dreams. The key to making this emotional motivator work is to find out what dreams the people in your market tend to share. Let me give you ideas that can help you see how this applies to your marketing.

One of the dreams shared by a large percentage of my market is to become a millionaire. I discovered this by asking many questions about why my clients wanted to master the art of marketing.

They wanted the marketing skills so that they could create a business that would help them become a millionaire. While not every single person in my market shares this dream, it became clear to me that the vast majority do.

What other kinds of dreams do people have?

What do they really want?

Can you position your product or service as the vehicle to help them realize their dreams?

Research in the area of psychology shows people want many of the same things. They want to look great and to feel better about themselves, but they want it without having to work too hard to get it.

If you were to study the vast majority of infomercials on television today, you'd find that they tend to cater to the dreams of the mass market. You'll see infomercials for diet products (look great), exercise gear (look great/feel great), and all kinds of devices to make life easier in some way.

For many years, I watched very little on television other than infomercials. I did this because my passion was marketing and the infomercial is a program that is end-to-end marketing. The more often the infomercial is on the air, the more successful that particular show is. That meant the more I'd pay attention to it.

❧ SUCCESS STRATEGY ❧

Your customers do know more than you. When you want to know how to grow your business, turn to your customers first. It is the most important step you can take. They know what they want or don't want. You must have this information to grow your business. Ask them for it and they will be happy to give you what you need.

You may or may not be marketing to the mass market. If you are, you probably have a huge marketing budget. For the rest of us who market to smaller, more defined markets, our job is to uncover the dreams shared by the majority of those in our market.

WHAT DOES YOUR MARKET DREAM ABOUT?

A great place to start your research is with your existing customers. Create a simple five-question survey and offer a small bonus item to every person who completes your survey. Here are three questions I might include on a survey:

1. Why did you really get involved in this business in the first place?
2. If everything goes as planned, what are you hoping to gain with your business?
3. What do you expect your business to do for you in the next year?

The outcome of the survey is to try to find a common goal or dream shared by most of your market.

When I asked my market why they got involved in their business, the overwhelming response was always "to make lots of money" and "to become a millionaire."

Armed with that information, it really wasn't all that hard for me to figure out what to do to properly promote my business to my market.

Here's an example outside of the business world. I have a client that owns a gourd farm. The farm is the largest provider of organically grown hard-shelled gourds in this country, and possibly the entire world.

To properly position this farm in their market, a little research was in order. We put together a quick survey and asked a few hundred current customers what benefits they received from crafting gourds. (These gourds are not edible. They are dried and last for decades so they are popular among artists and crafters.)

What we expected to hear and what we learned from doing this survey was eye opening. You are better off asking your market what benefit they get from your product instead of guessing what it might be. You have to step into their shoes and see things from their eyes. A survey is a very useful tool for this job.

What we expected to hear was that our market crafted gourds primarily for a hobby, or to fill some extra time they had on their hands. What the survey uncovered was that there were many in the market who crafted to sell their crafts to make money, and still others who crafted solely to win awards and gain recognition as a successful gourd artist.

We'd never have guessed these on our own, but they are important because of the number of people in this market who responded to our survey with these reasons for crafting gourds.

You'll need to do your own research with your specific market because there is no other way to really know what people want. And more often than not, I'm surprised at what we find from these little surveys of different markets.

No matter how experienced or how successful a marketer you are today, or someday become, there is no way you could ever guess what any market wants and hit it right 100 percent of the time. The best marketers never try to guess and always do their own research.

What you think people want is based on your background, experience, and beliefs and may or may not be in sync with what your market really wants.

Thus, many businesses miss the effortless moneymaking approach in their marketing altogether. Instead of asking a few simple questions to find out what their market really wants, the company assumes everybody wants to pay the least amount possible, so they market solely on a price basis.

I could write an entire book on pricing alone, but price is *not* the only reason people buy things. If it were, everybody would be in a perpetual price war and at the end of the day everybody would be out of business.

Research has clearly shown that price alone figures into a purchasing decision less than 10 percent of the time. It's *not* just low prices that people want.

Many times, in working with clients, I've doubled, and even tripled their prices overnight with no warning to their clients. Instead of killing sales, it actually increased sales. You must understand this point to be a success in business.

I've sold the exact same mentor program at $750 (followed by incremental price increases from $995 to $4,995) and now at $7,500 with hardly a ding in the number of sales I make each month. This is a 10-fold increase in price and sales have stayed steady.

It's not about price alone. It's about the dream. It's about having a life filled with joy and happiness—free from worry, fear, and illness. When you can show your prospects exactly how buying and using what you offer will help give them what they really want, they will usually pay whatever it is you ask of them, without question.

How did I increase my prices 10-fold and not hurt sales? I made sure they understood what they were buying. I wasn't selling a web site and mentor program. Instead, I sold them their dream. I sold them a system that could help them become an Internet millionaire.

With that picture firmly embossed in their mind, the price issue goes away. I could raise my prices to $10,000, or even $25,000 and still make a similar number of sales. And within a very short period of time, my prices will climb once again.

Stick with the dream *the customer* already holds in her mind and wants to realize. This is the power of this emotional motivator and why you must do all you can to determine the customer's dream and how your product or service can help her achieve it.

Let's go back to an earlier example in this book of the bottle of diet pills for a moment. You'll remember that the diet pills on their own are, well, rather boring. You could talk about what's in them until you're blue in the face, but few people will really care.

To make them sexy in the eyes of your prospect, you have to seek out those hidden benefits that can be linked to the emotional motivators and bring those to the forefront of your marketing every chance you get.

What do you think a person who takes diet pills can accomplish in terms of making a dream come true?

Taking the pills and losing weight might help a person in your market realize their dream of fitting into their favorite pair of jeans. If many people in your particular market have that as their dream, you could use that in your marketing.

A bigger, perhaps more universal dream for people who are overweight might be to have more energy to do the things they really want to do in life. Maybe they need the extra energy to keep up with their kids or grandkids. Maybe they need it to play their favorite sport such as golf, tennis, or jogging.

By asking the right questions of your market, you'll find out about their dreams and then your job becomes very simple. Show them how, through the direct benefit of losing weight, and the indirect benefit of having more energy, they can achieve their dream of doing more of what they truly enjoy.

THE DREAMS SHARED BY MANY

In the broad sense of using this emotional motivator, you could stick with some of the universal dreams that people have. These would include things like owning a nice house located in a nice area.

It might include having millions of dollars in the bank and not having to work any longer for anybody, ever. It may include being able to retire early, or very early. It may be traveling, at will, to any destination they choose.

People may dream of having great health, a stress-free life, and a life where work was optional, not required. Again, you can see these dreams being addressed clearly when you tune in to most any infomercial program.

Our desire to have our dreams realized is an emotional desire that tends to override much of our logic when it comes time to make a buying decision. This is why this emotional motivator, along with the previous four discussed in this book are so powerful to your marketing efforts.

When you pay attention to why people make purchasing decisions, you begin to notice how few times these decisions are made logically.

I've seen people in my own family who buy things out of emotion and have a difficult time explaining their true motives for making the purchase because the only explanation other people will accept is a logical one.

If you approached family and friends about their reasons for buying something, you'd expect a logical answer, not an emotional answer. The truth is that most people can't express the emotions that motivated their purchase.

They may know the emotional reasons for making the purchase, but they won't tell you what they were because they fear that you'll make fun of them, or they may hold any other number of such fears, so they remain quiet.

TRY THIS AT HOME

Do this little experiment for yourself. First promise to be completely honest with your answers otherwise there is no point to this whole exercise. Think about something you bought in the past 30 days. When you have it in your mind, ask yourself what you expected from this purchase.

In the past 30 days, I bought a new laptop computer. I could go on and on about why I bought the laptop and tell you it was for business reasons and that it has more memory and more power than my last laptop. I could get you to believe these are the reasons I invested in this new piece of equipment.

If I were to be completely honest about why I bought this new laptop computer, I would tell you that I bought it because I had a dream of being more productive by avoiding some of the issues I was facing with my old laptop computer.

But that's really still not the whole story. I bought *this* particular model for a much more personal a reason than a business reason. I like my freedom and don't like to be tied to my office to get my work done.

Hence, my dream was to have a powerful computer that would allow me to manage my business from anywhere. I could connect to the Internet while sitting on the beach, or having lunch at a local café and have plenty of power and storage so that I could carry every file and piece of software with me. Then I would not be tied to the office and could have the freedom to roam as I choose and work when and where I want.

This particular model offered me the chance to make that dream a reality because of what it offered in terms of power, size, and battery life. So I bought the computer, or more accurately bought the vehicle that would allow my dream of being free from the office to come true.

It's no mystery that you see many ads today for laptop computers that portray this exact image. The companies that make these kinds of computers know whom they are selling to and why their customers buy laptop computers instead of desktop computers.

The important thing for you to get from this example is that the product or service itself is in fact minimized in the mind of your prospect and the idea of the product or service as a vehicle to realizing a dream is amplified.

This can be a hard one for the person who created the product or who delivers the service to accept, but it's how massive numbers of sales are made using emotional reasons instead of logical reasons.

Now it's your turn. Why did you really buy what you bought? Get past the logical answers and see if you can figure out where your purchase fits in the grander dream you hold for yourself.

Part of my grander dream is to be on the road speaking at more seminars. My choice of this particular laptop computer fit well with my vision for my immediate future. It helped me to realize both an immediate dream and fit into an even bigger dream I hold for myself.

It was an easy decision because it fit with two of my dreams. When I read the marketing materials for this particular model, some of these elements were mentioned and it made it easy for me to see how this brand and model really did fit with my dreams.

Does this mean that no other laptop could fit my dream? Absolutely not! If I were to compare laptops feature by feature, I may well have found a better, faster, cheaper model. But the marketing is what sold me. The competition was selling their computers with a bullet list of features and nothing more.

If you ever wonder why some of the best products out there never get anywhere on the market, look no further than the marketing. Some companies spend all their energy on research and development and by the time they are ready to do their marketing, they settle for a bullet list of features and hope for the best.

The successful company looks beyond the features, does some research to find out what their market really wants, and then creates their marketing to show the customer how she can have realize her dream when she buys their products or uses their services.

Great marketing is no accident. You can have great marketing for your company if you're willing to do the things that great marketing is made from. It's really that simple.

Success in business depends on great marketing, so if you hold the dream of making millions in your business, buy my advice and make your marketing great, not just adequate. (Yes, I can be hired to help you with your marketing challenges!)

Unfortunately, this message may be lost on far too many people who look for the easy way out—which rarely ends up being the easy way out and often results in more pain for the business owner. Over time, that business may go out of business, be sold, or just continue to barely break even each month, thus aging its owners with undue stress and worry.

All this is because companies refuse to invest in their own market research and create marketing materials that motivate people to buy now. I beg you to see the light here and do all you can to get the best, most effective marketing materials created for your business now.

People decide to buy, or not to buy, based on their emotions. This is how most people make any purchasing decision in their lives. It usually has little to do with the logical side of things, no matter how much you may think it does. The mistake most marketers make is in thinking that they can lead with the logical stuff in their marketing and they'll make millions in sales.

Look at the most successful marketing campaigns out there and you'll immediately see they are not logical. Most campaigns are emotionally based and this is why you *must* incorporate the five emotional motivators in your marketing materials.

SAMPLE KEYWORDS AND PHRASES TO USE

- Live your dream.
- Own the house of your dreams.
- Meet the woman/man of your dreams.
- The solution you've been dreaming about is here.
- You can have it all.
- You don't have to wait to retire.
- Run your business from the beach.
- Turn your dreams into reality.

Let's look at how these five emotional motivators come together to create powerful marketing.

Creating Your First Emotional Motivator Ad

et's shift our attention to using the five emotional motivators in an advertisement. We'll call this your first motivational marketing ad. Before we do that, let's review the five emotional motivators to refresh your memory.

1. FEAR

People will take action when they fear the consequences of not taking action. The more fear you can build into your advertising, the more response you'll receive for your marketing efforts.

2. LOVE

Involving three levels of person-to-person connection, this motivator is powerful because of the way we are becoming more and more disconnected from one another. We now have more ways to communicate with one another than at any time in history, but we are now also a socially disconnected society.

When you can clearly demonstrate how your product or service offering can help connect people, you'll have a winning, motivational marketing piece.

3. FREEBIES AND BARGAINS

Who doesn't want to save money or get something for nothing? This is one of the easiest emotional motivators to integrate into your marketing materials, and it's very effective at getting people to respond to your marketing efforts.

Giving something away for lead generation purposes or as a loss leader to get people to respond to your advertising is a great way to use freebies. Creating a sale and chopping a percentage or dollar amount off an existing product is another powerful emotional motivator that will cause people to respond immediately.

4. EFFORTLESS MONEYMAKING

We've all probably responded to an effortless moneymaking ad at least once or more often than we'd like to admit. As a society, we've become a push-button, do-little, expect-a-lot-in-return bunch. It's a powerful emotional motivator to show people how owning what you're offering can help them either make or save money.

The key to making this really work is to make sure that it's effortless. If it requires your prospect to work (or exert effort) to make money, you'll not see much of a bounce in response to your marketing materials. Make it easy and effortless and people will respond by the thousands to your marketing efforts.

5. MAKING DREAMS COME TRUE

Everybody has dreams about how they want to look and feel, what they want to do, who they want to become, and where they'd like to go in life. Finding out which dreams are shared by the majority of your market and then aligning your products or services to demonstrate the connection between your offer and their dreams, leads to a dramatic increase in response to your marketing efforts.

THE IMPORTANCE OF GREAT MARKETING

You've probably started to think about how powerful some of these emotional motivators are and maybe you've even begun to fit them into your current marketing efforts. That is great; however, few people will ever take what I just shared and apply it to their marketing efforts, no matter how powerful it may be. There is a part of human nature that just refuses to believe that something that seems so simple can really make that much difference.

In many years of teaching this material to seminar participants who have paid thousands of dollars to attend my events, I could probably count on one hand the number who actually implemented what I shared with them.

They get excited about it all, take careful notes, and ask great questions, but somehow the distance between the hotel seminar room and their creation of marketing material causes them to lose their way.

I know your workload and life get in the way, but the key to get past this is to realize one fact: There is *nothing* you can do in your business that will be more *profitable* to you than investing your time in the area of *marketing*.

I know there are fires to put out, employees to counsel, and bills to pay, but there has never been an employee anywhere that is as interested in your success with your business as you are. You've got to take charge of your business, find time, and create powerful marketing materials for your business.

When I speak about finding time, I'm not speaking about using the last waning ounces of energy you might have before you go to bed to work on your marketing. If you do your marketing at this hour, how good is it really going to turn out?

Instead, plan to take some of your best, most productive time to work on your marketing materials. I'm most productive early in the day and again in mid-afternoon. During those times, I don't take phone calls, put out fires, or respond to e-mail.

Instead, I write sales letters, ads, web pages, e-mail marketing messages, auto responder messages, postcards, display ads, and so on. I use my best, most alert time to do the things that I know will result in the greatest income for my business.

If I waited until I was tired at the end of the day, my marketing would be mush—much like my brain is at that time of day. Then sales would decrease, and I'd be spending all my time trying to pull in a few sales here and there to try and keep the business alive.

This is how far too many people do it. They tell me there is no time to work outside the box on their marketing, so it never gets done—they continue to produce the same marketing year after year without revitalizing, revamping, or realizing what works and what doesn't.

Soon, these same people are caught in the trap that kills most businesses far too early. They work hard to keep the doors open and have no capacity, money, time, or energy to work on growing the business. They may be strong and last a few years, but they age rapidly and live with near-constant stress.

This is *not* what business is supposed to be about. It should be fun, profitable, and it should allow you to live the life you've always dreamed possible. This does not mean you have to work 80 to 100 hours a week, never get time off for a vacation, or risk ruining your relationship with your spouse because the business requires all of you.

The key to making a business successful beyond your wildest dreams lies in two areas. The first, a topic for another book, is your mindset. The second, the topic of this book, is your marketing.

If you're not already in the habit of reading books on success, I suggest you start buying some and read them. My library shelves are jammed to the point that there's not room for even one more book. There are no fiction books in my collection, just many business, marketing, motivation, and success books, all of which I've read at some point in my career.

I've trained my mind for success, and I've worked hard on my marketing materials. I still work hardest on my marketing materials when compared to everything else in my business. The reason is simple. My marketing materials are the tools I use to build my business.

If I were to plant a garden but I had no hose to water my plants, no weeding tool to remove the weeds, and no shovel to dig stuff up when needed, what kind of garden would I have?

If I had an automatic watering system in place, a gardener, and all the tools I could ever hope to have for my garden, what are my chances of success now?

Your marketing tools are the tools you use to grow a successful business. There is no other way to become a success in business. If you hope that people will just somehow find you, fall in love with you, and buy from you repeatedly for life on their own, you're in trouble.

However, if you realize that good marketing comes from taking the time to understand your market and to find out what they really want, on an emotional level—and you take the time to show them how what you have to offer will satisfy their emotional wants—you're likely to have a booming business in no time.

The good news is this is a choice you make. You can decide right now that you don't have time to create powerful marketing materials and make excuses to justify your decision, or you can decide that you *must* create powerful marketing materials if you want to live your life free of financial worry, fears, and hard work.

THE CHOICE IS YOURS

In a recent seminar where I was speaking, I met a fellow who had spent nearly $100,000 of his retirement fund on marketing programs. I was impressed that he was smart enough to invest in his marketing education as so few people ever do.

What really hurt was when he went on to explain that although he had spent all that money, he had not seen a dime's increase in his business. After further questioning him, I found out that most of the programs he had purchased were still sitting on the shelf, mostly with the shrink-wrap still unbroken.

This is what I like to call *shelf-help* and it's not going to make you any money. You have to tear off the shrink-wrap and wear out the CDs! Listen often; read until you get it. This book you're reading right now should be marked up, pages turned inside out, notes scribbled in the margins, and sections highlighted everywhere as you read it.

If you want a pristine copy for your bookshelves, go out and buy a second copy.

If you're just reading this book for entertainment, there's nothing wrong with that. Just don't complain that the motivational marketing strategies don't work. They work when you use them, but you have to master them first.

If you need to, go back and review each of the five emotional motivators now. This information will still be here when you get back and there is no race to finish this book and go on to the next one. The magic you're seeking is contained within the pages of this book.

What that means is you have all the goods on using the emotional motivators in your marketing right here in your hands. I can only hope that you use what I share and write to tell me about your success with it.

Your success is really what motivated me to write this book, for you. In sharing these powerful marketing strategies with you, I hope you take what you find in this book to heart and use it in your business.

PUTTING THE EMOTIONAL MOTIVATORS TOGETHER

Let's get back to motivational marketing and, more importantly how to use the emotional motivators for maximum impact.

To prove a simple point in my seminars, I make up a fictional product on the spot and ask the audience to raise their hands when I present them with an emotional reason to convince them to buy this fictional product.

I discuss each motivator individually, and different people raise their hands for different motivators. Finally, after I have covered all five emotional motivators, everybody in the room has raised a hand at least once.

This exercise is to illustrate that while using any one of the five emotional motivators increases response to your advertising, the real power of the emotional motivators comes when you begin to combine them in the same marketing piece.

While each is powerful on its own, not everybody wants something for free. Nor is everybody looking for effortless ways to make more money. Not everybody is easily moved by fear, or even by the need to connect with more people.

Our goal as marketers is to move as many people as possible to respond to our advertising and marketing messages. This is how we get the maximum mileage for our marketing dollars.

From this point forward, start thinking of how you can incorporate, at minimum, one of the emotional motivators in your marketing communications and, at the maximum, all five emotional motivators.

You will get more out of your market with the emotional motivators firmly implanted in your marketing materials. Response will jump, usually with the very first attempt. Over a longer time, you'll significantly increase the size of your business without necessarily increasing the size of your marketing expenditures.

A simple example of this would be a business that is sending an e-mail marketing newsletter to a market of about 30,000 people. Each week, they may send out an e-mail message and get back some orders because people have read and responded to the offer that was included with the newsletter. The cost of preparing and sending their weekly e-mail remains pretty consistent from week to week.

The person writing the newsletter spends about the same amount of time each week writing the content, formatting it, and getting it edited and ready to be mailed to their list of 30,000 subscribers.

While there may be no real cost to send that weekly e-mail to their list, there is a cost in labor to create the messages that are sent out.

By adding the emotional motivators into their newsletter, what changes? Does it cost any more to create that weekly newsletter? Is the person writing the copy spending any more time writing, editing, and formatting than they did before? Not likely.

The cost of sending the e-mail also remains the same. The only difference on the front end is that more thought goes into finding ways to integrate the emotional motivators into the newsletter. Don't worry, this will quickly become second nature to the person writing the newsletter.

So dollar for dollar, you're not looking at any measurable increase in costs to integrate the emotional motivators into your marketing. This is just one example using e-mail as the marketing channel, but it holds true for classified, display, radio, and television ads.

When you hit the correct emotional motivators for your particular market, the result will be nothing less than magical in terms of the sales you'll see. I've worked with many clients who have experienced this sales explosion and it truly is magical.

One of my clients found the magic emotional formula for selling men's hair replacement products by tapping into the dream that all men who have lost their hair share. The dream was to have a full head of hair once again.

They ran 30-minute infomercials on television that were literally little more than a stream of testimonials from men who were now living the dream of once again having a full head of hair.

They showed some men swimming, out on a date with a beautiful woman, or in a suit at an important business meeting. They were able to tap into the emotional want of their market and the business grew more than 30 percent a year for decades.

Imagine for a moment what it would be like for you to open your e-mail tomorrow morning and find not one or two orders in there, but instead you find 500 to 900 orders! How would that really feel? Would that excite you? Is it enough to motivate you to do everything you can to integrate the emotional motivators into your marketing materials?

I hope you're motivated, but you may be the kind of person who needs to see and feel things before you believe them. This may be one time that you'll have to trust your gut instincts and run with it to see if it will work. Maybe another story might help you see how powerful these emotional motivators really are. (I wrote this entire book about them—that has to tell you something!)

A TALE OF A COMPUTER TRAINER TURNED SUPER MARKETER

Not that long ago, I met a man with a dream. He had spent most of his career working as a high-level programmer for a large corporation and now, after nearly 40 years on the job, he wanted to build his own business.

This man had no experience in business and really didn't even know the meaning of the word marketing, let alone know anything about marketing or advertising. He truly impressed me with his knowledge of his craft and I suspect that he was in the top 5 percent of those in his industry.

His dream was to create a school where he could train people to become certified computer network engineers. He had some money, so he invested in an office suite, computers, desks, and one ad. He placed the same ad in the same newspaper week after week.

This was all the "marketing" he did to build his business and it simply wasn't working. To him, running this single ad was "marketing," and he was doing what the newspaper sales representative suggested.

In his mind, the issue wasn't marketing, because he was doing that. Instead he thought his lack of success had to do with things like the quality of the course, the manuals, or the software. While there is truth to some of that, putting all his attention on these issues was not helpful, and it is what most unsuccessful business owners do first.

A better approach is to put energy into perfecting the marketing. This is how you get people to your business in the first place. Nobody was going to see the quality of this man's course if he didn't fix his marketing.

After about a year of doing nothing more than running a single ad each week, he was able to attract, at most, six students into any one of his classes. This was well short of the goals he had set for himself, and at best, it allowed him to keep the doors to his business open and not much more.

When I met with him, I realized his issue was not with the quality of what he was teaching. What he taught was better than any of his competitors because he had such a passion for his work. It was a pleasure to watch him speak about his business and about what he did with the students he had managed to attract. They were in good hands.

He was a true master of his craft. This is true of many business owners I meet who are outstanding at what they do, but really are lost when it comes to marketing. The result is usually few clients, little profit, and a business that lasts only short time. You can't master every aspect of your business, and if you find yourself in a position where you're the de facto expert at what you do but can't seem to attract a single new client, it may be time you seek out help with your marketing.

With my client, I had to do some research to figure out which of the emotional motivators his market would respond to. My client didn't want to invest another penny in his advertising, so whatever I did to help him had to be done within the existing advertising budget. Sometimes you can solve marketing issues by tossing more money at the problem, but in this case, there was no more money to toss around. I accepted the challenge.

Do Your Research

Since I knew nothing about this man's market, I started right at the beginning. I had no idea why people choose one computer training school over another. I had never been in a position to even explore that kind of training for myself. Where do you begin to look when you're trying to find out just what emotional motivators will work best with your market? Begin with your existing customers.

This is what I did with my computer school client. I asked for the names of 10 people who had recently enrolled in his school. This was hard because he only had five students at that time.

But just asking those who had already enrolled in the school didn't give me the whole picture, and this might be true in your case as well. I further asked for the names and phone numbers of 10 people who had chosen *not* to enroll in his school. This was much easier since he had a list of those who had come to meet him, yet ultimately decided to enroll at a competing school.

The next step was to pick up the phone. You have to call people and speak to them if you want answers to your questions. So that's what I did.

Set aside uninterrupted time to make calls to move your business forward. There is no easier, more effective way to get this job done. Set aside the time and get it done. Do not procrastinate. You'll find it's much easier to jump right in than it is to dip in one toe at a time.

But getting on the phone wasn't all I did. I also wanted to find out what the competition was up to. Why do people choose the competition over you? What emotional button or buttons is your competition hitting that you missed with your marketing materials?

You may go as far as calling your competition, as a prospective customer, just to see how they handle your inquiry. This is how I did it with this client's competitors. What I found out gave me a lot of information about what was needed to bring my client into the big leagues.

When you shop the competition, see how they greet you, treat you, and motivate you to make a purchase. Pay close attention to how they get you excited about coming back again. If you want to compete effectively, you have to know what the other side is doing that you're not.

Instead of fearing your competition, look to them as a place to learn more about your market and the people you sell to. Stop thinking that the other people who sell in your market are taking business away from you (and that makes you mad). They are another business offering similar products or services. You'll do yourself a great service with this simple change in thinking.

The truth is that no matter how similar they may be to you, they are anything but an exact copy of your business. That means that some people will choose to frequent them over you, and vice versa. There is no real competition because, in business, we all offer products and services that differ from others in the market.

If you come to my seminars, you'll get marketing advice you can use. If you attend somebody else's seminar, you'll get marketing advice you can use. It may be similar, but it is not the same. We really don't compete in the true sense of the word.

This is indeed true even if you are offering the exact same product as another company. If it's not the product, it might be the service that's different, or the store layout, location, or look and feel, the pricing, and so on.

Consider letting go of the belief that there is any real direct competition out there. It'll make a nice difference to you and your business.

FIND OUT WHAT THE COMPETITION IS DOING

Research opens your eyes to what's going on out there in a way that you normally can't see. I began to look at the computer school market to find out who else was in that market and what they did to promote their businesses.

The easiest thing to do was look at where my client was already advertising his business. As it turned out, each week he was investing $500 to place a small display ad in the local newspaper under the heading of "Computer Training."

I was sure his market was looking in that section to find places to get their training because two other schools were also advertising in that same spot in the same newspaper, also every single week. These other two schools were my client's "competitors."

Here's what was interesting about them. The largest school placed the biggest ad each week, typically three times as large as my client's ad. So you could guess this big school was getting the most exposure, or at least getting noticed first.

The second school also had an ad in that same newspaper, just below that of the largest school in this market. The ad was smaller, but still larger than the one my client was placing each week.

Would simply placing a larger ad do the trick? If you spoke to the advertising rep of the newspaper, I'm sure that's what you'd be told. It's only part of the issue, and just buying a larger ad is no guarantee of increased sales. You could still have a message that does not motivate your prospects, only now it costs you more and is bigger.

Just looking at these ads did not give me enough information to act on. I had to do some more market research. This time, I called the two other schools and acted as if I was interested in enrolling as a student with them.

PUTTING THE PIECES TOGETHER

After doing my homework with the people who did enroll, those who didn't enroll, and calling on the two other similar schools in this market, I had the information I needed to put into effect a powerful motivational marketing ad using the emotional motivators.

Take notes here because this is what I discovered. First, of the three schools in this market, my client's school was priced the lowest, by a wide margin. Yet he was having trouble enrolling students. Was price the issue that needed to be fixed?

While many people believe marketing means selling at the lowest possible price, that's simply not true. The price you put on your products or services figures into a purchasing decision less than 10 percent of the time. Unfortunately, for far too many business owners, marketing means lowering your prices and nothing more. Rarely do I advocate a company lower its prices to increase sales because it's a losing proposition over the long term.

The other schools offered financing, an offer my client was not in a position to make to his prospective students, so I kept asking questions.

The biggest school was set up with an experienced sales team that followed up repeatedly after my inquiry. I knew this was a huge advantage over my client, who was his own sales team and spoke with an Indian accent that often made it hard to understand what he was saying.

The second largest school also had a sales team, but they only followed up once. This may have explained why they were the number two school on the list instead of the number one school.

When I went back to look at the pricing each school had for what was essentially the same education, the picture began to come into focus. The largest school, with the powerful sales team and large advertising budget, also had the highest prices. They were charging $10,000 for this specialized computer education.

The second largest school was charging less, but still substantially more than my client was asking for the same course.

They were at the $7,500 price point, which compared well with the largest school in the area. They were a little more moderately priced, had a smaller ad budget, and a less professional sales team, so it all made sense.

My client, however, was charging a mere $1,500 for the same computer training. If price were the issue, this would be the missing piece that tied it all together. I guessed that I might be right about my client's pricing being far too low when compared to the other schools in his market.

The fact that my client was very likely the most qualified of anybody teaching at any of these schools at the time was not reflected in his pricing. Like many business owners, he bought into the idea that to be a success, you have to charge the lowest possible price you can afford to and still stay in business. No, we're not all Wal-Mart!

It didn't work. He was hurting for money each month and the business he started to enjoy his life more was just adding stress, fear, and challenges to his life.

After careful consideration, I floated the idea that my client raise his prices to at least be at par with the second largest school in his market. The look of absolute fear on his face told me that he'd never agree to it. Like so many business owners, his price was based on what he thought he was worth in the marketplace. This goes back to self-valuation or self-esteem issues, which are topics for another book. He simply did not have high self-esteem and hence was severely undercharging for his superior educational offerings.

So how was I going to help this man if he was not willing to raise his prices?

To increase this client's business, I had to raise his prices because he was not seen in this market as a serious contender. Yet my client would not agree to increase his fees. Price was the issue to be dealt with.

There is one emotional motivator that is price-centric, and that's the one I decided to use. The emotional motivator that deals with price is the one that speaks about getting something for free or at a bargain price.

A Marketing Idea that Turned a Business Around

The job at hand was actually quite simple. All that was required was to increase the price of the computer training and then hit on one of the five emotional motivators using the exact same ad space my client was already buying each week.

First, I looked at the headline in my client's ad. It read, simply, "Computer Training." The ad was placed under the column header above the three computer schools' ads that also read "Computer Training."

I suppose my client had let the newspaper create his ad and when you take that approach, you typically get an ad made by an amateur. Creating advertising for some is a full time career, but if you work with most publications, it's usually the graphics person, who also happens to create ads, who ends up putting your ad together. This is not a winning formula.

It's much better to hire this sort of thing out and get an advertising or marketing person to create your ads for you instead. Yes, it costs more, but you'll make it up 10-fold in the response your ad generates.

An ad with a horrible headline is certainly not going to produce great results, so start with a better headline. Whenever possible, integrate at least one of the emotional motivators into your headline.

In true marketing form, I transformed my client's headline from dead to deadly. And in a single brush stroke, raised the price he was charging to be comparable to the second largest school in his market, then I used the "bargain" emotional motivator to solve two problems.

First, my client wanted no part of charging $7,500 for his program. To him it was just too much money. It was far too much of a stretch for him to jump from $1,500 to $7,500 overnight. Second, people in the market were buying on price, so what we charged for the training really did make a difference.

The ad he placed in the newspaper each week went from having a headline of "Computer Training" to a headline that read, "Half-Price Sale."

The magic here was that we were now within range, price wise, when compared to the other schools in this marketplace. Second, we were able to sell the training for half of what the second largest school charged, which made my client very happy.

I changed nothing else in the ad. The copy was the same, the layout was the same, and the typeface and size were the same. All that was changed was the headline.

The ad still cost $500 a week to run because it was the same size, only the headline was changed.

THE AVALANCHE

The new ad came out on a Wednesday of the following week. I waited a day before trying to reach my client. When I did try to call, his line was busy. So I tried again, still busy. Finally, at around 7:00 P.M., I got the phone to ring and on the other end a weak voice answered.

This new ad, with only a headline shift had generated a literal avalanche of calls. I can only wonder just how many people could *not* get through who really wanted to enroll in his school.

My suggestion was to get people in there immediately to help handle the phones, to add more phone lines, and figure out a new way to enroll as many people as possible.

This was an exciting time, but also a time when some businesses would crash and burn. Too much business in too short a period of time can be just as devastating as too little business. Using motivational marketing techniques, several businesses have gone out of business due to the explosion in response they got from their advertising efforts.

This did not happen in the case of the computer school. He was able to get more phone lines in and immediately hired two salespeople to help him handle the influx of calls.

He continued to run this very same ad week after week and the response stayed very strong. Within 90 days, he had reached his capacity and had to rent out another office suite twice the size to accommodate his growing school.

He also hired three additional trainers, and added courses until his calendar was full six days a week. Within six months, he rented a third location and was well on his way to making his first million dollars—doing what he loved most.

Is all this possible with just the changing of a single headline? It is! To know just what to change in your headline, you have to know which of the emotional motivators is going to have the greatest impact on your market.

If you follow the steps outlined in this book, you will be happy with the results.

Let's look at how we can use the emotional motivators in a sales letter.

Motivational Marketing: Sales Letter Strategies

I n Chapter 9, I showed you how to use emotional motivators in an ad. In this chapter, we'll look at using the emotional motivators in a headline. This is important because it's a proven fact that the headline may well be the most important part of any marketing piece.

Consider what most people do when they read a newspaper. Do they read the story or the headline first? Before deciding whether or not to invest the time to read the story, most of us read the headline.

When it comes to advertising, the same thing applies. People will read the headline in your ad and decide whether to continue reading. Many marketers believe that the headline is as much as 80 percent of the power of any marketing piece.

Using the wrong headline means that very few people will read the rest of your ad, and you won't see many sales. However, if you have a great headline, more people will read your ad, and you'll see more sales as a result.

The best part about headlines is that simply by changing a headline, you could dramatically affect the results of your advertising. I've seen business owners get as much as a 700 percent boost by doing nothing more than changing the words they use in their headline.

As you read in Chapter 9, the headline was what made all the difference in the results a computer training school received from the owner's advertising efforts. Headlines occur in every marketing or communication piece you create, regardless of the media you choose to use.

In a simple two-line classified ad, the headline is very short. It's usually no longer than two or three words. You'll usually see those initial words printed in **BOLD CAPS**. The goal is to get the reader to stop and look at your ad. When most people read classified ads, they rarely read every ad.

Instead, people tend to scan the ads and look for something that catches their attention. They are looking for an emotional button that captures their attention and entices them to read the rest of the ad. One simple classified ad that I've used successfully for years incorporates an emotional motivator in the headline, and others in the body of the ad.

Read this simple ad and see if you can pick out at least two emotional motivators:

> **FREE E-BOOK.** Discover the secrets of making money on the Internet. Get your copy now. Go to http://www. UltimateWealth.com.

This little ad has been responsible for building my prospect database and has run in publications ranging from *USA Today, Entrepreneur* magazine, and *Investor's Business Daily,* to hundreds of online publications. I've used this ad successfully for almost a decade.

This short ad works because the headline is an attention-grabber. It hits on a powerful emotional motivator—getting something for free. The reader immediately feels as if there is a gift waiting for him, which makes him feel good, and he will circle this ad or set it aside and visit my web site as soon as possible.

If you caught onto this emotional motivator, congratulations! It's great to know you're paying attention. There is another emotional motivator that may or may not be immediately apparent to you if you don't know the market in which this ad runs.

The market that will see this ad is the market of people who are looking for ways to build a successful business on the Internet. Many people dream of finding a strategy that will make all the difference and turn them into millionaires overnight.

Some of them spend large sums of money following this dream. But you wouldn't know this unless you've done your research into this market and discovered exactly what emotion drives the customer to spend money. Once you have this information, it's easy to push the buyer's emotional buttons and get him to respond.

The second emotional motivator in the ad is "dreams come true." What's the dream? The dream is being able to discover a "secret" that will make all the difference. But that's not all this ad offers. Look a little deeper.

What does the secret help you do? Make money. Is that another emotional motivator? Could it be that combining money-making with the idea of a "secret" translates as a way to get easy money?

Of course, it does! This one tiny ad touches on three emotional motivators. Is it any wonder that this ad has worked so well for almost a decade already? And it will continue to work well for as long as it continues to be published.

ADS DON'T HAVE TO BE COMPLICATED TO WORK: UPGRADE YOUR STRATEGY

Simple ads work. They work even better when you can incorporate emotional motivators into the ad itself. These tools get people to stop, feel, and respond. During my career, I've successfully used classified ads for just about every one of my clients, typically with great success.

The size of the ad does not always matter, but the emotional buttons the ad pushes that get people to respond do matter. This is often contrary to what you'll hear from the ad reps at the newspapers and magazines.

If you run an ad that doesn't work, the first solution the ad reps have for you is to make the same ad bigger, invest more money, and try again next issue. An ad that isn't working isn't going to suddenly work better because it's bigger! This is not a solution to your problem, it's a solution to the ad rep's problem of increasing advertising revenue for the publication and, in turn, his sales commission.

However, if you have a classified ad that's working, you can indeed make it bigger, and it may very well increase your response rates.

Perhaps the best advertising strategy you can use is what can be referred to as the *upgrade strategy*. Here's how it works. You begin with the smallest ad you can get, which is the classified ad.

These low-cost ads are published quickly, and they won't break the bank if they fail to produce the results you had hoped for. The best part of classified ads is that you can also publish them on the Internet and you'll know whether you have a winning ad in about 24 hours.

This is the fastest way to get out there, test, get results, and refine your ad for the next test. Yes, you have to test, refine, and retest your ads until you find a winner. This is the unwritten rule in marketing. Many people try an ad once and if it doesn't work, they go on to something else.

This is like giving up digging when you're only inches from finding all the gold. It's not the way to create a successful business. A better way is to stick with it until you discover the correct formula for your market. When you do, you'll appreciate the fact that you stayed the course because the results will be fast and profitable.

The foundation of the upgrade strategy is that you stick with it until you've found a winning formula. Once you have a winning formula, then you can upgrade to the next level of marketing. This is what it looks like for many of my clients.

First, they begin with simple classified ads and refine their message until they find the emotional motivators that get the best response. Some clients will test all the emotional motivators, do their research, and test multiple ads at the same time with the single goal of creating an ad that gets the most response possible.

Second, they will print the successful classified ad on a postcard and mail it. If the classified ad formula works, it will also work as a postcard. They may also choose to run the same classified ad copy in the same newspaper or magazine they used for their classified ad, only this time as a larger display ad.

Again, the results will be better since more people will see their message. Third, they may decide to take the same basic message to radio or television. These steps allow a company to become successful without blowing all their money on advertising.

You may want to go right to television with your very first ad, but testing it in a medium that costs dozens of times more than classified ads can cost you your business. Far too many would-be successful businesses ended up giving a television station all their money without being able to get enough re-sponse to cover their investment in the advertising. You don't want this to happen.

Use the upgrade strategy. Yes, it takes a while to get your message to the level of being on television, but once you do get there, you'll have the confidence that people will respond to your message, and they will.

THE POWER OF A SALES LETTER

Much has been made of the sales letter both from the positive and the negative side. In my own experience, I know of no other tool that packs as much marketing punch as a sales letter.

Once created, a sales letter can work for you for years and even decades. It's the most versatile of all marketing pieces, and it's a powerful marketing piece for most products and services.

Let's be clear about what this marketing piece is and what it is not. It is a long-form marketing piece that will aver-age 10 or more pages in length. It is not a few short para-graphs cobbled together in the hopes that it will do the job of selling.

The power of the sales letter comes from its ability to inform, educate, and motivate a prospect into making a purchase. During the course of the sales letter, it directly addresses every possible objection and turns it into a positive reason for purchasing.

The sales letter is long because it takes many words to han-dle every imaginable objection, to build trust and rapport, and to motivate a prospect to buy what the sales letter is selling.

Picture this in your mind: You're standing in front of your prospect and you're eager to make a sale. But your prospect is skeptical and has a lot of objections that you must overcome be-fore their credit card comes out. If you're there in person, you can expend the effort required to make that one sale. You may also soon discover that making sales in this way just isn't effective because of the time it takes.

The sales letter, in my view, is a sales presentation in print. It performs the job of the in-person salesperson many times over, usually reaching hundreds or thousands of prospects simultaneously.

The sales letter is indeed a powerful marketing tool, but magic happens when you take that same sales letter and incorporate the five emotional motivators. Sales letters that produced nothing can start to produce incredible profits. Sales letters that produce good results can easily begin producing stellar results. And sales letters that were already doing well, become world-class sales letters by any measure.

The sales letter is typically filled with stories and metaphors to help your prospect gain a clear understanding of why they really want to purchase what you're offering. This process takes time to accomplish and that's why sales letters end up being fairly long.

❧ SUCCESS STRATEGY ❧

Whenever you can, be sure to use word pictures in your sales letters. As you write, paint pictures in your prospects' minds so they can "see" what you're saying. Couple these word pictures with emotion and you'll have a powerful combination working for you that works exceptionally well at making sales.

Do long sales letters sell better than short sales letters? I've often heard it said that long sales letters far outperform shorter letters, but I wanted to test this theory for myself. A few years ago, I had a 10-page sales letter that was selling 10 people out of about every 1,000 that would see the letter on my web site.

At the time, I had a friend who was also involved in marketing and I asked if she would help me reduce the length of this sales letter so that I could test it to find out if a shorter letter would be better than a longer letter. After much editing, we managed to get the letter down to about three pages. We kept just the facts and main points and removed all the other stuff, making it a very tight and direct sales letter.

When we tested it, the first 1,000 people to see it bought nothing. So we left it on the web site a little while longer and the next 1,000 also bought nothing. Maybe this was a fluke of some sort, so we waited it out a while longer to see what would happen.

After about 5,000 hits and no sales, I placed the long 10-page sales letter back on the web site and sales started coming in again. During this experiment, I would have made about 50 sales with my long 10-page sales letter.

Lesson learned. Long sales letters sell. From that point forward, I've only used long sales letters on my web sites and in my direct mail campaigns. Now keep in mind that a live presentation on a teleseminar, web cast, or live seminar is still a form of a sales letter.

When you consider how many ways you can use the sales letter, it's easy to see what a powerful marketing tool it can be for your business. Now let's look at how to integrate the five emotional motivators into your sales letters.

THE POWER OF STORIES

In all the years I've been writing sales letters, the one strategy that has produced the best results is the use of illustrative stories in my sales letters. As humans, we're captivated by stories. We want to know what happens, and if the story is at all interesting, we'll put everything else aside and stay with it until it ends.

As an illustration of just how much some of us are attracted to stories, I recently saw a lady walking down the aisles of a grocery store pushing her shopping cart *and* reading a book at the same time. She was so caught up in the story in her book, she could not put it down! This is the power of a great story, and it's why you absolutely want to integrate stories into your sales letters.

Another great example of storytelling is in the media. What do we call news reports? "Now with the story, here's Bill . . ."

Even the media uses stories. No matter which media you're talking about, stories are the foundational method through which information is conveyed. If you've ever read the Bible, you'll note that it too is composed mostly of stories and within the stories are the lessons the story seeks to convey.

Does this mean your sales letter has to be as long as a book? Of course it doesn't, but you should use your sales letter to both entertain and educate before enticing your prospects into purchasing what you have to offer.

The magic of these stories happens when you pay attention to the emotional motivators and you hit them all in your sales letter. Let's look at the main parts of your sales letter so that you have a clear understanding of what's contained in this powerful sales tool.

COMPOSITION OF A SALES LETTER

GRAB THEIR ATTENTION

When you read the newspaper, you know what you read first, right? It's the headline. This is the tool that grabs your reader's attention, causing the reader to decide whether they even want to read your sales letter.

Spend a lot of your time crafting and testing your headline. It's not a bad idea to write out 100 or more variations of your headline and test the top five until you find the winner in the bunch.

This is not an easy thing for most marketers, but the most successful marketers take the time to test, test, and retest. Everybody else expects to hit a home run on the first try. Good luck with that approach.

Using emotional motivators in your headlines captures the customer's attention the fastest and gets more people to read your headlines than anything else you can say or do.

BUILD RAPPORT

Once you start writing your sales letter, the very first paragraph has to be one that solidly connects to your reader. To make this happen, you have to be very clear on who your market is and what problem or issue you can solve for them.

For example, if I were writing a sales letter targeting chiropractors and I found out that the biggest challenge they have is attracting more patients to their practice, I would directly address this issue in the very first paragraph.

If I were also a chiropractor, it would be written in the first person, and if not, it would be written in the third person. Here is what that opening paragraph might look like:

> When I first opened the doors to my new practice, I had visions of people lining up around the block waiting to see me. It came as quite a shock to me that after six months, I had only a handful of patients, was out of money, and had no idea how I was going to keep the doors open for even one more month.

The idea is to align your offer with the issue faced by the person in your market. In this example, my offer would be to help the chiropractor get new patients with a new program I've created or through a consulting relationship.

Notice that closing the sale does indeed begin right at the start of any sales letter. If you use this one concept, it is a snap to close the sale at the end of your letter because you've been closing since you began the letter!

The first part of your sales letter is going to say "I understand your problem" or "I had the same problem(s) you now face." This is how you build rapport.

Once the prospect gets the message that you understand what she is facing, she will be many times more likely to read the rest of your letter and, most important, place an order with you for what you're offering.

This initial paragraph can also serve as the lead-in to the story or stories you're going to share later on in your sales letter.

TELL A STORY

Although I'm not advocating that you write tales of lore in your sales letters, they do share many of the same elements. A great way to see this visually is to think about how a Hollywood movie tells a story. Do they paint lots of pretty pictures? Do they embellish the basic story? Is the movie ever the same as the book?

In the movies, they do what they need to do to get you engaged in the story. You do the same thing in your sales letters. If you are successful at emotionally enrolling your prospect in your story, you dramatically increase the chances he or she will read the entire letter and ultimately buy from you.

To do this effectively, you're going to use both the direct and indirect benefits of your product or service that also hit on the five emotional motivators. A person selling diet pills might write a letter starting with the fact that at one point he, too, was overweight.

The person might embellish his story with all the things that were painful in his life when he was overweight. Then, he can introduce the product, and quickly shift back to the story of what happened when the weight came off.

Maybe he could show a photo of himself and his new love snuggling up together. He could share the story of how his self-esteem has increased and what happened next.

Tell a story of success and, as you do, weave in the emotional motivators. In this way, you captivate your reader, hitting their emotional buttons and, at the same time, helping them to see themselves in the story. They may be overweight and have low self-esteem, but they can see their life changing for the better just like the person in the story. All the writer has to do is let the buyer know what to do next.

MAKE THE CLOSE

This part of the sales letter is often misunderstood, so I'll do my best to share with you what a close is and why it's the icing on the cake when creating a sales letter.

During your sales letter, you've likely now related emotionally driven stories of success with your product or service. If you don't yet have any of these stories, please get them. Even if you have to give away a few hundred units to friends and family, you must have success stories in your sales letter.

A great strategy to get more success stories fast is to offer the product to your best customers for free in exchange for their written testimonial. You may even wish to go a step further and ask them to appear in a video or get permission to record their voice for future use on the radio. You'll be surprised just how quickly people jump at this opportunity.

Keep in mind that you cannot, under any circumstance, fabricate your testimonials. While it may be tempting and certainly easier to do that, it could land you in a lot of trouble if you're ever asked to prove your testimonials are in fact true and written by real people who are not attached to your company in any way.

As a rule, I keep the original copy of all the testimonials I've ever collected. If I'm ever asked, it's just a matter of searching through several piles of binders to find the original testimonial, signed by the person who wrote it and giving me permission to use it.

Testimonial stories serve as the foundation in the creation of your marketing materials, so they are important to both collect and manage. When you're ready to use them, it's important that you can find them quickly and easily. Your time is much better invested in crafting your sales letters instead of trying to remember where you put that cocktail napkin with a testimonial scribbled on it!

The best way I've found to collect testimonials has been to create forms with the specific questions I want people to answer already spelled out. From there, I'm almost assured of getting the kind of testimonials I can use in my various marketing materials.

In the close, shift gears from a motivator to a marketer. The close is where you can (1) weave in some additional bonus items to satisfy the emotional desire to get something for free, (2) drop the price to satisfy the need to get something at a bargain price, and (3) drive home the emotional points you've previously illustrated in the testimonial stories in your sales letter.

If you've done this right, the close won't be difficult because by the time your reader arrives at this point, she is already motivated to buy from you. The only real time you need an overly powerful close is when you have a weak sales letter that did not push any emotional buttons and has left the reader on the fence about ordering.

When you do push the five emotional motivators, you'll often find that your prospects have long ago made the decision to buy; they just need the close to find out what to do next in order to get your product or service.

The important part of the close in your sales letter is to give your prospects as many ways to order as possible. When a person is emotionally engaged, he wants what you've got to offer right now. If you can deliver your product electronically, great. If not, be sure to offer overnight shipping and priority processing to cut down the delay between your customer placing his order and receiving the product.

One other thing to consider is offering as many ways to order as you can think of. This includes ordering online, faxing, calling a toll-free phone number, and ordering by mail. Also offer as many ways to ship your orders as you can think of because some people have certain preferences to as how they want their order to arrive.

The goal in all of this is to make it easy for people to order they way they are comfortable ordering. There's no point in exciting a person and then telling them they can only order on your web site and shipping will take four to six weeks. I promise you, many people will pass on the offer to buy from you.

Marketing is really nothing more than making it easy for people to give you their money in exchange for your products or services. Your job is to make it as easy as humanly possible for this exchange to occur.

It's easy to see this in action when you think back to any sales letter you've read in the past that compelled you to place an order for the product or service that was being offered. These are the letters you want to file away because if you bought from that letter, the odds are pretty good that many other people did too. A letter like this would make a great model to follow when it comes time to craft your own sales letters.

Many marketers maintain files of sales letters, ads, articles, and more that they refer back to time and again. This is the best way to really learn how to craft sales letters that sell.

Take those formats and add in the emotional motivators wrapped into testimonial-style stories and what you'll end up with is a sales letter you can use again and again for decades. Did I mention that you'll probably love the profits you'll reap from such a letter as well? You will!

❧ SUCCESS STRATEGY ❧

When you close your sales letter, be sure to sign your name. This is important because your prospect wants to know who wrote the letter. When you do sign your signature, however, use your Hollywood signature, not your legal signature.

To see some examples of this in action, visit my main web site at www.UltimateWealth.com. The sales letters I use on this web site are filled with motivational marketing strategies and would make a great addition to your own files.

Be sure to grab all the free e-books offered on the site, too, because they are marketing pieces jammed with motivational marketing. And also be sure to visit www.MotivationalMarketing.com for even more resources you can use now to create powerful, emotionally charged marketing pieces.

In Chapter 11, we look at using the emotional motivators in your Internet marketing efforts.

11

Motivational Marketing: Web Site Strategies

L et's take motivational marketing to the Internet. After all, where is there more marketing activity than on the web these days? Since the online world began, marketers have been trying and testing every imaginable piece of technology to get people to buy from them.

While technology can indeed be addicting and seductive, by itself it's not enough to convert prospects into paying customers. Many times I've been asked to look at a person's brand new web site—the result of tens of thousands of dollars invested for every techno bell and whistle ever created.

While many of these kinds of sites are pretty to look at and often fun to play with, they are complete and total disasters when it comes to marketing. These sites are generally the result of somebody being seduced by the technology and losing all sight of what's really important—making the sale.

This can come as shock to the person who's just invested every last dime to have her web site professionally designed and developed, only to later realize that the site was built by a person who had great technical or graphics skills, but who knew nothing about marketing.

For many years, I've argued that the web sites that make the most money are rarely the most technically advanced. What separates web sites that sell from those that just look pretty is the content on the site.

If you visit a web site that shoves all sorts of technical bells and whistles between you and the content, the odds are very good that you're going to pass on that web site and click on the next link, which usually takes you to the competition's web site instead.

Your prospects are no different from you and they will do the same thing with your web site unless you make it easy and fast for them to get what they came for.

PAY-PER-CLICK SEARCH ENGINES

Where do you start on the Internet when you're using motivational marketing? Begin where you're going to advertise to attract people to your web site. The biggest market for finding new prospects on the Internet is through the major search engines.

For many years, the search engines provided free indexing of your web site, but that all began to change at the start of the new millennium. Today, search engines make their money selling clicks to an advertiser's web site.

A printed publication charges you a fee to advertise based on how many people could possibly see your ad. They get this number by determining how many copies of the newspaper or magazine will be printed and distributed. They may also enhance this number by telling you that although actual printing and distribution is one number, readership is three to five times as high.

Maybe I'm not paying attention, but how often do you share a magazine with a friend? If readership were really that much higher than distribution, everybody who gets a copy of a particular magazine or newspaper would need to share it with three to five other people. It doesn't happen.

You end up paying a higher price to advertise based on an inflated number. A more accurate assessment, in my opinion, is to take the total distribution, or total number of copies printed, and divide that number in half.

Since there is no way to know how many people will really see your ad in any printed publication, it's hard to know exactly what a fair price for an ad is.

The online world saw this problem and created a great solution that seemed to solve the distribution and readership number debate. Instead of paying for a hypothetical number of viewers to your ad, you now only pay when somebody actually clicks on your ad.

You pay for results instead of just the number of people who may see your ad. This arrangement has truly upset the balance in the advertising world as more and more advertising dollars find their way to the Internet, leaving fewer and fewer dollars for the print world.

Like many others, you'll probably use a lot of pay-per-click (PPC) advertising to promote your business and make the Internet an integral part of your marketing efforts.

Pay-per-click advertising is really nothing more than an electronic classified ad. To get a feel for what I mean, log onto the Internet and surf over to your favorite search engine. What I'm sure you'll find are ads either at the top or on the right-hand side of your screen that are usually identified as "Sponsored Ads."

You buy sponsored ads when you use PPC search engines. These ads are very similar to the classified ads we spoke about in a previous chapter. In fact, the same motivational marketing strategies apply here as they do when creating classified ads that will be run in print publications.

The first line of your PPC ad is really your headline. This is where you'll capture a reader's attention and get them to stop and read the rest of your ad. The rest of the ad is the offer and the call to action.

The following example is a classified ad that I've been using for years:

FREE E-BOOK. Discover the secrets of making money on the Internet. Get your copy now. Go to http://www. UltimateWealth.com.

This same ad has also been used very successfully with PPC search engines. This works in the same manner online as it does offline because, while many people are caught up the technology of the online world, you have to remember that on the other side of that Internet connection, there is a person. Just like you, they too have thoughts, feelings, and emotions.

The Internet is *not* about being a new media or a destination. It is simply another channel by which a business can reach out to prospects and convert them into paying customers. Much of what you do in your offline marketing will also apply when marketing online.

You can use the classified ad you created for use in newspapers and magazines for your PPC advertising efforts. You'll still use the first two words as your headline, the body to pique curiosity, and the call to action to direct the reader to the next step.

The difference with the online world is that you'll only pay when a person actually clicks on your ad, not for the estimated number of viewers. Some ads you'll run will be displayed more than 20,000 times and will receive only a single click. So you'll only pay for that one click and not the 20,000 impressions your ad has had.

Now, if you're getting that low of a click-through rate, maybe you want to go back in and have a look at your ad. It may not be doing what you want it to do.

The great thing about marketing online is that you have immediate access to the kind of detailed information you need to find out whether or not your advertising is working. And you are always allowed to go back in and change or update your ad at any time, for any reason. This is something that is not possible with printed publications. Use it to your advantage.

It's a great idea to check your ads at least once a week, or more often if time allows. It's also a good idea to make changes to your ads one item at a time. You may have the headline correct, but something else in your ad is just not working. You'll never know that unless you only make one change at a time.

Many times, just by changing the headline of your PPC ad, you'll be able to dramatically increase your response rates.

❧ SUCCESS STRATEGY ❧

Your headline either works or it doesn't. Getting just a few clicks here and there means your headline is not working. You'll know when you have a winning headline because of the response you receive when your ad runs.

Although it's beyond the scope of this book to talk about PPC advertising strategies, I wanted you to understand that this is a very viable method of advertising and all signs now show that this form of advertising will continue to be viable for some time to come. Use it to your advantage!

YOUR WEB SITE

You can use PPC advertising to drive people to your web site, so let's look at how to use motivational marketing to make more sales.

First, I want to share a brief note about using PPC ads to bring people to your web site and getting them to stay. If I were to use the earlier ad and offer people the opportunity to grab a free e-book, but once they came to my web site, they had to search for the free e-book, they will more than likely leave.

Some people mistakenly think they can just use any old hook to bring people to their web sites and that's enough. It's not. I have gone so far as to create different landing pages for each ad that I run in the PPC search engines.

You must make sure that (because you are promising a free e-book in your ad) when a person clicks on your ad the first thing he sees is how to get the free e-book. When advertising multiple offers, have a different landing page for each PPC ad you create.

People have a very short attention span when they surf the Internet and more often than not will not spend even 30 seconds looking for a link buried on your page to get what they came to get.

One effective strategy is to mirror the exact same headline you've used in your ad on the landing page where you direct people when they click on your ad.

If I said "Free E-Book" in my PPC ad, when the prospect clicks on my ad and comes to my web site, I want to make sure that the headline on that page also says, "Free E-Book."

This makes the prospect feel certain that they've arrived at the correct web site. This is such a simple strategy and it works so well that I find it amazing more marketers don't use it. You should.

In Chapter 10, we looked at creating sales letters for direct mail use. On the Internet, those same sales letters can be used very effectively to close sales from your web site.

The same people who will read a sales letter that you sent in the mail will also read it on your web site. And the same strategies apply with just a few minor changes.

Long sales letters sell, and this holds true on the Internet as well. If you look around, you'll see that some of the most profitable web sites use long sales letters to sell their products and services.

Keep a long sales letter on the same web page rather than breaking it up into segments across many pages. Many people prefer not to read on a computer and will instead print out your sales letter and read it offline. If it's broken up over several pages, it is harder for your prospect to print it all out.

What you may also find is that if you break up your sales letter over multiple pages, your prospects will not click through all the pages before leaving your web site. This is something you don't want to have happen.

Unlike printed sales letters, you can use color as much as you'd like on the Internet. Consider making the headline of your sales letter appear in bold red type across the top of your web page.

Some web developers will tell you that red clashes with their designs and that you'd be better off using fuchsia for your headline. Don't do it! Stick with red and then stick to simple black type on a white background for the rest of your sales letter.

It's not a design masterpiece, but your job is to make more sales, not win design awards with your web site. If you must, it's worth going to battle with your web designer over this issue. If it means firing your web designer, do it.

If there is one battle we all face in this business, it's dealing with people who see things through the filter of design, color, and layout, as opposed to seeing things from a marketing or, more important, a people perspective.

You can never lose sight of the fact that what you're doing on your web site is motivating people to buy from you. This requires that you remove every possible barrier (technical and otherwise) that can get in the way of you reaching your goals.

In 1995, I began teaching people how to market on the Internet. At that time, I realized that a big hurdle for many business owners was that they had no idea how to use the technology and more often than not, the technology got in the way of them being able to market effectively.

To make sure that never happened in any of my seminars, there were never any computers in the room. (Imagine coming to an Internet marketing seminar and not seeing a single computer in the room.) The reason is simple. Start with what you know. Participants at my seminars always had access to legal pads and pens. This was technology they knew how to use and it did not interfere with their creative process.

From there, they were told to use only the technology needed to achieve the result they desired. Most of them realized that the level of technical help they needed really was little more than what a typical high schooler could do.

So instead of investing tens of thousands of dollars to develop a web site, they instead spent hundreds of dollars and got what they really needed to make sales on the Internet.

The power here is that you can use the same sales letter on the Internet as you do in your direct mail efforts. If you wanted to, you can even use the same sales letter and create it as an e-book you can give away on your web site too.

CREATING A FREE E-BOOK

Creating an e-book that you give away on your web site for free is a powerful marketing strategy that I have used successfully for more than a decade.

You begin to build your free e-book giveaway by creating a small classified ad that you use in both print publications and with PPC search engines.

You could use the classified ad I showed you earlier as a model for creating your own classified ad. Always start with a powerful headline that uses at least one of the emotional motivators. The most common headline for this kind of ad is simply: "Free e-Book!"

The body of the ad would hit on another emotional motivator by offering a powerful direct or indirect benefit offered by the e-book. Here are some examples of what you might write:

✔ Discover 10 effortless tips for losing weight while you sleep.
✔ Regain your youthful energy in as little as 30 days.
✔ Uncover the secret marketing strategy that will turn any web site into an automatic cash machine.

You get the idea. The body copy hits on an emotional level and gets your prospect excited about clicking the link in your PPC ad.

The ad is then linked to a page that expands on the benefits of the e-book being offered. It's easy to think that it's enough to offer the e-book and just have a simple form to capture a name and e-mail address, but here too, you have to build up the value of your e-book in your prospect's mind or she will not request it, even if it is free.

You're asking people to trust you with their name and e-mail address, so you have to make it worth their while. A short four- to five-paragraph sales letter explaining the benefits offered in your free e-book will do the trick.

When your prospect opens your e-book, it too must be in line with the ad and the landing page you sent her to. Keep the topic and headline exactly the same or very close to the same so she knows she downloaded the correct e-book. Remember, your prospect requested and downloaded your e-book because of what you promised in your headline. If you fail to deliver on that promise immediately, your prospect will simply delete your e-book from her computer.

The e-book in this case is your sales letter. When your prospects read your e-book, and the testimonials in it, they will be compelled to come back to your web site to place their order.

The great thing about the Internet is that you can then follow up with these prospects via e-mail using an auto-responder message sequence, and you'll convert more of your prospects into paying customers.

ONLINE ORDERING

Where things become different than the offline world of direct mail is in the ordering process. There are entire books written on how to properly create order forms and how to write copy for your forms. Again, you will use the emotional motivators in your order form.

You'll do great if you use your order form as a place to reiterate the top three to five benefits of owning your product or using your service. A great idea is to reserve writing the order form section until you're fresh and full of energy. If you've just written a 10-page sales letter, wait a day or so before writing the order form.

The order form often gets little attention because it's the last thing people do. By then, they are tired and just want to be done with their marketing piece. You can choose to either write the order form first, or you can choose to write it a few days later when you're reenergized.

When your prospect hits your order form, it's decision time for him. What seems to happen far too often is that a prospect will come to an order form and decide not to place his order. This happens even after he reads your 26-page sales letter and gets all excited about making the purchase.

To alleviate this all-too-common issue, be sure to bring back your top three to five emotional motivators on your order form. Here's an example:

> _____ *YES, Robert, I'm ready to discover the Secrets to making money on the Internet. I realize your program can immediately help me go from zero to millions in as little as two hours per week. I also understand that if I'm not completely satisfied, I can return everything for a prompt refund, no questions asked.*

This is a fictitious product, but the idea is that you hit those emotional buttons once again in the order form—just as you did in the initial PPC ad that got them to read the sales letter you filled with stories that hit these same emotional buttons.

You can see that you really never stop hitting the emotional motivators once you uncover those that work best for your market. To get the most mileage out of the emotional motivators, you would ideally also have a letter that is sent out with the product to once again hit those emotional buttons. This will help assure that the sale will stick and you won't be making many refunds.

Remember that an emotional sale must be reinforced as often as possible. It's a little like saying, "I love you" often to your significant other to keep the fire alive in your relationship. Your customers need to be reminded often why they made the decision to buy from you.

Try adding a thank-you letter to every order you ship to your customers and remind them of the emotional benefits they will receive when they begin to use your product or service and see how quickly your refund rates begin to drop.

This again is yet another simple marketing strategy that most companies never get around to doing. How often have you received a package that had only the product you ordered and nothing more? There was no thank-you letter reinforcing your decision to make the purchase in the first place and certainly no start to a long-term business relationship.

You could build a business on one-time-only sales, but why would you want to? It's so much easier to build your business with a list of people who buy from you again and again and who love doing business with you.

Take the time to build relationships with your prospects and customers. It's worth the extra time and effort it takes because you'll be rewarded with many more sales and much more profit in the years to come.

12

Motivational Marketing: Display and Print Advertising Strategies

Can you still use motivational marketing strategies if you're a traditional marketer using display and print advertising in printed publications and do very little on the Internet? You sure can! Let's see how it's done.

Display advertising is the next level up from classified advertising in the print world. With a classified ad, you generally use only words in your ad. You're also charged by the word to run your ad in that particular publication.

With display and print advertising, you now introduce the new elements into your ads, including graphics, photos, and a variety of typeface choices. While this can give you creative flexibility, these additional elements can keep you from staying focused on the most important part of your ad—the copy.

Often in this type of advertising, you're going to be tempted to work with a printed publication's graphics person who will be more than happy to create a work of art for you to run in their publication. While this may sound like a great idea, run, don't walk, away from this offer.

This entire book is dedicated to creating advertising that gets people to respond. I've never met a graphic artist who has a great gift for marketing. Marketing is *not* their primary skill set, so expecting them to create an ad that gets outstanding results is a mistake.

You'll often end up with something that looks really great, but that rarely does what you expect it to do. Graphics people focus on the part of the process they've been trained to focus on—color, layout, balance, design, and so on.

There is indeed a time and place for these skills, and it's usually later in the game—*after* you've written the copy for your ad. In my own business, I rarely use a graphic designer for my display ads. I have fought with them for far too many years over how my ads should look in order to get the maximum response from my advertising efforts.

❧ SUCCESS STRATEGY ❧

When you place your ad in a printed publication, request that your ad run on the right-hand side of the right-hand page. This is the first place people's eyes go to as they turn the page and it's the best place for your display ad to be placed in a publication.

ADVERTORIALS

Ads don't have to look good to work. This is even more true when you incorporate emotional motivators into your copy.

One advertising strategy that follows this train of thought, and that I really love, is an *advertorial,* or a combination of an advertisement and an editorial. An advertorial looks like another article in the publication, usually in the same format and typeface as the other articles and the only difference is the word "Advertisement" printed at the very top or bottom of the page.

The goal here is to get the reader to read an ad that is cleverly disguised as an article. The format works like magic. When you begin to use the emotional motivators in an advertorial, there is no better display ad format you can buy at any price.

There are certain challenges with this type of advertising. First, it's hard to get the publication to agree to run an advertorial because they tend to feel it fools the viewer into reading ad copy that looks like editorial copy. This is the point and it's the reason why this format works so well.

I often wonder when I hear a publication denying the use of advertorials in their publication if they are interested in their advertisers succeeding with their advertising. But I'm coming from a marketing perspective that primarily sees response as the most important part of advertising and I could be wrong.

The second challenge is that you'll often be asked to buy a full page in the publication at a cost of tens of thousands of dollars. If you're going to disguise your ad as editorial copy, you're going to need at least a full page. Be prepared to lay out the funds for this type of display ad purchase.

You could choose to run a quarter-page advertorial instead of a full-page ad and make it look very much like the editorial copy in the publication, but since your space is limited, it is much harder to get this size advertorial to work.

Many larger companies run advertorials in some of the biggest magazines in the country, and they run several, or even a dozen or more pages, in a single issue. Pay attention to these ads when you come across them as they can serve as a great model for you to follow.

You'll also find a lot of advertorials today in some of the big news magazines like *Time, Newsweek,* and in more niche publications like *Golf Digest* and *Popular Science.* Companies using advertorials include electronics companies, such as Bose and Sharper Image, or companies that market sporting goods.

When you spot these advertorials, rip them out of the magazine and immediately put them in your *swipe file* (i.e., a file to keep your favorite ads, articles, sales letters, and more for later reference).

It's perfectly fine to borrow ideas from these ads. Rarely do you start with a blank sheet of paper when it is time to create an ad or sales letter. This is a very common practice among those in the marketing community.

If a company already thought of and created a marketing technique that you like and think might work for you, borrow the idea and create your own ad based on their concept. As you get more familiar with this industry, you'll see the same strategies being used in different publications and get a good feel for what works and what doesn't.

Advertorials work. You've got about 300 or so words to work with, which allows you plenty of time to build on your emotional motivators. You can borrow some of the copy you've written for your sales letter and incorporate it into your advertorial.

ADVERTORIAL STRATEGY

As with all your marketing efforts, you've got to have a strategy before you invest your first dime in anything. One of the most effective strategies for advertorials is to create a "drooling demand" for something you're going to give away free as a lead generator. This is commonly referred to as a "Hand-Raiser."

Your entire advertorial, instead of trying to sell anything, should instead be designed to get your reader excited about getting something you're offering free. You might offer free reports, free e-books, free audio CDs, free software, free trials, or even free DVDs. Remember, "getting something free" is a powerful emotional motivator.

Use the free item to do the selling for you instead of using the advertorial to sell. This is important because even with 300 or more words of copy, there is still not enough space for you to build your case, gain trust, build up your offer, drop the price, and close the deal. While many marketers try to do all of this in one ad, they soon find out it can't be done in a way that is cost effective.

Look at some advertorials and see how they structure their content and what they are offering. Often you'll see what is known as a *soft offer*, offering something for free or something at a very low or introductory price.

The goal here is really twofold. First, as people respond to your advertorial, you'll add them to your prospect list, which then allows you to market to them over and over again for years to come. Next, you'll be sending them something that will be much more substantial in terms of being able to make the sale.

One strategy I've used successfully is to offer a free audio CD in my advertising. The respondent is asked to visit a web site or call a toll-free number to claim their free audio CD. There is no charge for the CD, which has a face value of $97, however, the respondent is asked to pay a small shipping and handling fee, typically $6.95.

The secret to making this strategy work is that all of your expenses are actually covered in the small $6.95 shipping and handling fee, effectively making this a zero-cost marketing strategy.

The CD is a powerful marketing tool because it allows you to create an hour-long presentation that can end with a sales presentation directing the listener back to your web site or to a toll-free number to place an order. In a 60-minute period, you have more than enough time to make your case and close the sale.

Within that period, you have plenty of time to hit every emotional motivator several times with different stories and illustrations to increase the number of sales your audio CD brings in.

Once you have an audio presentation that you can deliver and you know gets results, you'll need to turn that same presentation into an audio CD, and use every form of advertising to give those CDs away as fast as you can.

Marketing is indeed a numbers game. It's important to get people responding to your advertising so that you can send your follow-up marketing materials to improve the number of sales that come from your marketing efforts.

One of the most successful companies that uses a similar formula is Video Professor. This company built their entire empire by giving away a free CD with a sampling of their programs. This one strategy turned a small company into a behemoth in just a few years.

I've received free DVDs or CDs from companies such as DR Field Brush Mowers and Sony. Big companies use this strategy because it works and it's one you should consider in your own business, too.

CREATING TRADITIONAL DISPLAY AND PRINT ADVERTISING

Often you will run ads that fall under the category of *traditional* advertising, instead of the advertorial, which is considered a hybrid advertisement. With more traditional advertising, you'll be tempted to include photos and maybe some other design elements as well.

As is true with all advertising, including advertorials, you begin with a powerful headline to stop your readers and make them want to read your advertisement. A compelling headline is the most important part of your advertisement, so it is under-stood that you should spend as much time as possible creating the most compelling headline you can create.

From the beginning of this book, I suggested you test head-lines in your classified ads and on the Internet, where it's both cheap and fast to test. By the time you create your first display ad, you'd normally have a headline that you've tested many times and have proven to work.

You can, and probably should, be testing headlines in every possible way. Begin with the lowest cost media first, then move up to postcard mailings to test some more. By the time you're ready for a display ad, you won't have to guess what you should use for a headline because you'll already have several that you know work.

Your graphic artist may want to diminish the headline in your display ad because it makes the ad look "out of balance" or you may hear him tell you the headline "sticks out like a sore thumb." This is what you *want* the headline to do!

If the headline doesn't literally jump up off the page and grab your reader's attention it doesn't matter what words you use, she will never see it. While this type of approach may make your graphic artist's stomach turn, it works and that's why you want to fight to make sure your ad design has a big, bold headline.

A common mistake is to hire the publication to create your ad. It's usually a disaster. The publication knows who is paying the bill for the ad, so they will print the name of your company in big bold letters across the top of the ad where you'd really want your headline to appear. What is motivational about your company name? A few years ago, I had a company create a booth for me at a business trade show. They did what I just shared with you. Along the top of the booth, there was the name of my com-pany, Ultimate Wealth, Inc. in big bold red letters about 12 inches tall.

Impressive, I thought for a moment, this is *my* company finally making a statement. I quickly came to my senses and put myself in the shoes of the person walking up the aisles of a trade show. What is the primary question on his mind as he looked at booth after booth?

It certainly wasn't "What's the name of your business." Instead, that person was asking, "What does this company do?" At every single booth, almost every visitor is trying first to understand what the company does, not what their name is.

It was well after midnight the night before the trade show, but I knew I would be in trouble if I didn't change what is essentially my headline on my trade show booth. I ran out to an all night copy place and made a truly ugly banner to replace the full-color, glossy banner the booth creation company had made for my booth.

The next morning, I had a brand new headline on my booth that looked one step above being written with a crayon, but it had much more impact. It answered the question my prospects already had in their head, "What does your company do."

The banner read, "Profitable Internet Marketing." It was ugly, but by the end of the trade show that day, my voice was really raw. I'd been speaking to as many as 50 people at a time all day long and never had a moment to run to the bathroom or grab a bite to eat.

What do you do? Profitable Internet Marketing. If you have a business, profitable internet marketing is important, and there is very good chance you're going to stop by to see what I can do for you.

The interesting part is that in all the trade shows I've attended, I've only seen this approach a handful of times in the tens of thousands of booths I've seen. It's the same thing in your display advertising. Your ad is out there in some magazine, but your prospect is thumbing through the pages asking, "So what?"

Your job is to answer the question already in her head with a headline that hits her on an emotional level. When you can effectively do that, you'll have many people stopping to read your ad.

Testing is the key to finding the correct emotional buttons to push. These buttons must answer the primary question your prospects are already asking. This one-two punch works like magic, but it's not always easy to find.

You know when you've stumbled onto such an ad because it will make you stop and read the ad. I once saw an ad with a headline that read "FREE DVD." It stopped me alright. I read the ad and responded to get my own copy of the free DVD that was being offered.

A recent headline in a daily newspaper read, "eBay Income the Easy Way." This full tabloid-size page probably cost the advertiser more than $30,000 to place. This ad would run once and last only one day.

When I see an ad like this in a daily newspaper, I assume it's working exceptionally well. I dug into this ad a little farther and found the company behind the ad. They were indeed doing exceptionally well and had ads on the radio with the same headline. They were also sending out direct mail pieces with the same headline. All of this combined was filling their seminars with hungry prospects.

PHOTOGRAPHS IN YOUR ADS

One of the fastest ways to hit many of the emotional motivators in your advertising is by the use of the correct photograph or photographs. After all, a picture is worth at least 1,000 words and, in the world of advertising, you need as many words as you can get!

Let me share an example of a typical ad you might find in any of the business opportunity magazines. The ad has a photo of a young couple, typically sitting by the ocean, which is bright aqua in color, suggesting they are on some Caribbean island.

The couple is shown gazing into each other's eyes, perhaps even leaning into one another. The photo shows a small table with the traditional Caribbean fruit-filled drink with a long straw and slice of pineapple hanging over the edge.

What is this image really saying to the viewer?

From an emotional standpoint there is a lot going on here. First, you can absolutely see the emotional motivator of connection in play. The couple is obviously close so there is a connection between them. You can take it further still and assume that they share a love for one another. If that's true, then maybe the emotional motivator of sex is also implied in this image.

What else might you get from this image from an emotional motivator standpoint?

You could conclude that this couple is making money while they play. So this would fit well with the emotional motivator of "easy money." While they are sitting out on the beach of this tropical paradise, their business is still making them money.

Is there more in this image? Certainly! Who else might dream of having the time and money to sit on an island enjoying paradise? Maybe it's a dream you hold for yourself. This hits on the emotional motivator of having your dreams come true.

Not everybody is going to share that dream, but for those that do, they will get the message. In this one image, you could essentially hit three of the five emotional motivators in the same ad.

If you're an overachiever, you'll want to find ways to hit the two remaining emotional motivators; fear and getting something free or for a bargain.

That's easy enough to do in the text. You can offer a free report, e-book, audio CD, DVD, or even a free trial. Then, to use the emotional motivator of "fear," you'd say something like "Only available while supplies last" or use a hard deadline at which time the offer expires.

What you end up with is what you might call the "Ultimate Motivational Marketing Ad." When you can hit all five emotional motivators in any ad, you've found a sure-fire way to hit a home run with your marketing.

Not everybody in your market will respond to the same emotional motivator. Some people will jump at the chance to get something for free. Others have no interest in getting even one more thing for free, but they will respond to making their dream of being able to vacation, at will, on a tropical island come true.

As a smart marketer, you want to always be sure to put as many motivators as you can find into a given ad to increase your chances of having more people respond to your advertising efforts.

Over the years, I've watched for the ads in magazines that would run as full-page ads month after month after month. I tore out these ads and looked to see how many of the emotional motivators they had in the ad. Almost every ad used all five emotional motivators in the same ad.

This is a clue that I paid close attention to early on. But seeing and doing are two very different things. Over the years, I've been testing ads with all five motivators in printed publications and on the Internet. In one sentence, these ads work great!

Take your full-page printed ad and make it into a web page. Can you see how this might work online, too? Now your only challenge is getting enough people to see your web page. In a printed publication, you're paying the publication to be able to get your message in front of their existing audience.

On the Internet, you have to bring the audience to your ad. This is why it can be a little bit of a misnomer to think that advertising on the Internet is free. Putting up a web site will cost you next to nothing, but the "currency" of the Internet is traffic.

A web site nobody ever sees will not make you any money. A web site that gets thousands of visits a day will make you rich, but you're going to have to pay somebody to get that traffic to your web site.

My preference is always to go where the traffic already exists rather than trying to bring the traffic to you. In the long run, you'll find this is a much more effective way to market that won't break the bank in the process.

Begin by asking yourself, "Who is already doing business with the people who buy what I have to sell?" This will give you an idea of where to look to find your market and what places you might choose to place your advertising.

Take the first step and find the publications and web sites your prospects read and visit. The next step is to call the publications and get them to send you a media kit. These are also typically available on the publication's web site.

You'll want to look for a few key items in the publication's media kit. First, you'll want to study the demographics of their readership because this will give you a nice overview of who is really reading their publication.

You'll also want to know how much they charge to place an ad with them. This information will be found on their rate card, which is always included in their media kit. Keep in mind these rates are negotiable, so never pay rate card prices for any of your advertising.

Finally, you'll also get a copy of one or two of the most recent editions of the publication. If you downloaded the media kit from a web site, just call the publication's advertising sales department and ask them to send you a copy of their current issue. They will be glad to do it.

When you get it, study all the ads in the publication.

What are they selling?

What are the companies that advertise in the publication offering?

You might even go one step further and call some of the companies advertising in the publication to see if you can get any information about how well the publication is working for the advertiser. You may be surprised by what you uncover.

While this procedure is not always fun, it's well worth the effort and it could save you thousands of otherwise wasted ad dollars if you uncover a publication that is not performing well. On the flip side, it'll help you to determine which publications are working great for other advertisers.

When an ad fails, the advertiser is quick to blame the publication, when, more often than not, it's the ad itself that may be at fault.

Now, let's look at using motivational marketing on the radio.

CHAPTER 13

Motivational Marketing: Radio Advertising Strategies

The best part about motivational marketing is that it can be used in every advertising channel. Radio is perhaps one of the most overlooked media channels for most advertisers. With great reach and good prices being just the start of a long list of reasons to use radio in your marketing mix, let's look at radio from a motivational marketing perspective.

To better understand the real power of radio, you have to first understand how human communication actually works. While we can get very excited about written words on a page, this is just the start of how we communicate. (The first two parts of the human communication model are covered in this chapter, but I save the third for Chapter 14.)

By themselves, the words represent 7 percent of the human communication model according to many neuro-linguistic programming professionals. While we can do a lot with words to bring in emotion, words by themselves are the just the beginning.

When you introduce the next portion of the communication model, including voice tone, inflection, volume, and speed, you now have an additional 38 percent of the human communication model.

Both words and voice quality are at work on the radio. In terms of numbers, you get 7 percent (words) plus the 38 percent (voice quality) of the communication model when you use verbal media to promote your business.

This combination makes radio a powerful media to work with. These same attributes are present when you market with audio CDs or voice over the Internet, but they are less potent marketing tools than radio advertising.

The reason is perception. If you were to send your prospect an audio CD, they would have one impression of you and your message. However, if you were to play that same exact presentation over the radio, the same prospect would have a completely different perspective of you and your company.

This is where the power of big media really lies. You can appear bigger than life when your message is presented on radio or television. So why do so many marketers not use radio? It may be they don't understand the true power of the medium.

Be aware that most radio stations would like to sell you what they want to sell you, but I want you to instead buy the best kind of airtime you can get from a radio station.

Over the past few years, radio stations have begun offering shorter and shorter spots for you to promote your business. While this may be a great way for the radio station to bring in more advertising revenue per hour, a 30-second spot on radio will probably not work. When you look at the copy for a 30-second spot, you'll find that you have about five lines of text.

This is akin to a long classified ad, only this time it's on radio airwaves. It's much easier to work with a 60-second spot, which used to be the standard in radio. With a 60-second spot, you have enough time to pique your prospect's interest and direct them to the next step. So when the radio station offers to sell you a bunch of 30-second spots, tell them what you really want are 60-second spots, and don't settle for less!

❧ SUCCESS STRATEGY ❧

Radio stations rarely sell all of their available airtime except during the peak holiday season. During the rest of the year, there are many bargains to be found, but you have to be persistent. If your ad is not date sensitive, it may be worth it for you to buy only unsold airtime for pennies on the dollar, even if it means your ad will run overnight.

INFOMERCIALS

One format in radio that is less well known, but which is a prime choice for a motivational marketer, is to buy 30 minutes of airtime (i.e., a 30-minute spot). Much like a television infomercial, the radio infomercial can be incredibly effective for many businesses.

The key to a radio infomercial is to do your homework and find out as much as you can about the type of people who listen to your chosen station or stations. For many businesses, going after a broad market is not effective, but if your product or service is well suited to a more general market, this format may be ideal.

Radio is a mass-market medium, so your message, to produce the best results, has to be more broadly focused. While this is not always possible, you can work with indirect emotional benefits to draw in people from the larger radio audience.

Let's say that you're offering a specific business service that many business owners need, but hate to invest in. What you might do is create a book, special report, e-book, audio CD, or DVD that addresses the issues of what might happen if the business is *not* protected.

Think of business insurance as an example. This is a product that business owners don't enjoy investing in, yet it's critical to their business. The best way to motivate the business owner is by painting a picture of what might happen to their business if they fail to have insurance protection.

You might create a report titled, "How to Avoid the Seven Most Common Mistakes Business Owners Make That Could Put You Out of Business Overnight." You can see how even a short 60-second spot might be good enough to motivate business owners to call you or visit your web site.

Once you've created this special report, which should be somewhat substantial in nature, you have the foundation for what might later become your 30-minute radio program. This report, to be of value to the end user, must have plenty of easy-to-understand meat in it that clearly presents you and/or your company as the de facto expert on the topic.

Think how you'd feel ordering a report that claims to help you avoid going out of business only to find out it's a single page, double-spaced, and is filled with industry lingo only a seasoned pro could understand. It won't work for you.

Pay somebody to create this report if you can't, or sit down with your favorite microphone and record it to an audio CD. This is a time when it's worth going the extra mile on a project. This is your first contact with your prospect and, as you know, you don't get a second chance to make a first impression. Put your best foot forward.

You might even follow my lead and suggest to your prospect that even if she doesn't choose to do business with you, she must still consider getting business insurance coverage. While you might think this is a horrible idea, remember, this book is about the psychology of why people buy.

How would you feel if I were to give you a great piece of advice and in the same breath let you know that you could hire me to do your project, or somebody else that you felt more comfortable with?

Think about it. How would you really feel?

Would you feel pressured in any way? Or would you feel even more compelled to hire me for your project? Most folks would not even think of working with anybody else when you open that door. It goes a long way in helping you grow your business, and it's something you should be in the habit of doing.

In this entire book, I did not cover "desperation" as an emotional motivator. It's not. Whenever you appear desperate or hungry to a prospect, it makes him wonder whether you're any good at what you do. He may ask himself, "Why is he or she hurting for business?"

Once this conversation starts in your prospect's mind, you've lost the game. So you suggest to your prospects that you're fine if they choose to work with somebody else or buy from another company. You send the message that you're so successful that there's a line of people waiting to do business with you.

This is a hard one to understand because it goes counter to what you might think, but it works. It's part of the psychology first discovered by Maxwell Maltz, author of *Psycho-Cybernetics,* that states that you "act as if" you are a success before you become a success.

This is a powerful tool for a business that is seeking to become much more successful than it is today. When you're a success, you don't mind giving up a little business here or there. By letting your prospects know you're fine with them buying from somebody else, you stand to gain much more than you'll ever lose.

You'll never capture 100 percent of the prospects you attract, but the hope is that you capture enough of them to make you wealthy. And it really doesn't take all that many prospects to create a million-dollar business.

RESPONSE TO A RADIO ADVERTISEMENT

When you use the radio to advertise, you have to keep in mind that your prospects only have one way to get your message— through their ears. They can't see your web address, read your company name, or rewind anything to hear your ad again. This can be tricky if you're not prepared.

Here's how you win on the radio in terms of getting response to your advertising. First, if you're going to send prospects to a web site, the domain you choose has to be radio friendly.

The person listening should be able to both retain and spell your domain easily because she will *not* be able to see it in writing anywhere. So you are in big trouble if you have a domain that looks like this: www.thebestwidegestinthewest.com/~www/temp/specials/offer33.htm.

Domain names are less than $10 today and you should get into the habit of securing as many easy-to-say and easy-to-remember domain names as you possibly can.

I recently secured the domain, www.TheNextMillionaire .com for my business. This is a great radio domain because the words are easy to remember and spell. If you're listening to the radio and you hear an ad that sends you to "The Next

Millionaire.com," you're very likely to remember the domain name when you can finally get to a computer.

Most of your radio audience is going to hear your ad while driving. They will *not* be able to write down your domain name or phone number, and they may not even remember your offer two minutes after your ad runs.

To overcome this issue, you'll want to also include a toll-free phone number in your radio advertising message. It is preferable to have a number that relates to a word, such as "1-800-FLOWERS." Again, your prospect is likely sitting in his car with nothing to write on.

❧ SUCCESS STRATEGY ❧

When looking for a radio-friendly domain on the Internet, start with the shortest domain name you can think of and then add one simple and related word to either the front or back of your first word. It may take a while, but this simple strategy has allowed me to secure many great domain names when others thought, "all the good names had been taken." It's not true. There are plenty of great domain names available, if you're willing to work at finding them. Also, be sure to check out eBay.com using the search term *Domain*. There are many sellers who offer great domains for sale on eBay. Your domain registration company may also sell expired domains or domains currently owned by other people who may be willing to sell them for a reasonable price. There is no reason why you should not have a radio-friendly domain name!

Include both a radio-friendly web address and radio-friendly toll-free phone number in your ads and be sure your toll-free number is answered 24 hours a day, seven days a week. Radio stations are known to air your spot in the middle of the night to fill in time they have not sold, so you want to be sure you'll capture those late-night leads. Normally, you won't pay for these overnight spots, but they can and will generate phone calls and visits to your web site, so you've got to be prepared.

MOTIVATIONAL RADIO ADVERTISING

One of the biggest issues you'll have with creating your radio spot is what to say in the 60 seconds to wow your prospects. At this point in your marketing, you should already have a well-tested emotionally driven headline. You should have tested it with classified ads, postcards, sales letters, and display ads. You can usually use the same headline in broadcast media, too. After all, it's just another media channel to get your message to your prospects. And your prospect is literally the same person who is motivated by the same emotions.

If people respond to your emotional headline in print, and on the web, they will respond on the airwaves, too. Just like in your classified ads, postcards, sales letters, and on your web site, you'll want to begin your radio ad with your headline.

This is the point at which a listener will decide whether to tune your ad out or to pay close attention to it. Your headline is the opening sentence in your radio ad and it must capture your prospect's attention.

If your headline fails, the rest of your ad will be ignored and you'll wonder why it didn't work. Often just changing your opening line can dramatically increase response to your offer, as it can in print and on the Internet.

If I were going to give away the free report I mentioned earlier, I might begin a radio spot by saying:

> Now you too can avoid the seven most common mistakes that could put you out of business overnight. Call right now to request your free report that details these deadly mistakes and how to avoid them. Absolutely no cost or obligation, and it could save your business from almost certain disaster. Call now, toll-free 1-800-333-FREE or visit us on the web at 333free.com.

While this is a fictitious example, it's representative of a script that works well on the radio. The only thing you would likely want to add are a few lines of additional emotional benefits to your prospects about why they want this report and why they must get it now.

I might add that this report is only available while supplies last or until a specific date in the near future. This adds the key element of urgency to your message, causing more people to respond. This is another way to the use the emotional motivator of fear to get your prospects to respond now.

You can fit all five emotional motivators inside of a 60-second radio ad if you work at it. Here's an example of our same 30-second ad now expanded to a 60-second radio ad:

> Now you too can avoid the seven most common mistakes that could put you out of business overnight. Discover how quickly and easy it is to put a system into place that will completely eliminate deadly mistakes and help you easily reap untold profits, in as little as 60 days. Thousands of business owners are already using our system. Isn't it time you joined them to make your dream of owning a profitable business a reality today? Call right now to request your free report. Absolutely no cost or obligation, and it could save your business from almost certain disaster. Call now, toll-free 1-800-333-FREE or visit us on the web at 333free.com. This offer ends Friday at midnight. Call now!

See if you can spot how many of the five emotional motivators are included in this simple 60-second ad (*hint:* they all are):

1. Fear
   - ✔ Can avoid the seven most common mistakes.
   - ✔ Eliminate mistakes.
   - ✔ This offer ends Friday at midnight.
2. Love
   - ✔ Thousands of business owners.
   - ✔ You joined them.
3. Freebies and bargains
   - ✔ Free report.
   - ✔ Absolutely no cost or obligation.
   - ✔ Call now, toll-free.
4. Effortless moneymaking
   - ✔ Easily reap untold profits.
5. Dreams come true
   - ✔ Make your dream of owning a profitable business a reality today.

This is a simple example of how it might look when you create your own script. Just remember to think about the person you're trying to reach and what it is they respond to emotionally.

If you opt instead to run a full 30-minute show, you should hit all five emotional motivators as often as three to seven times during the 30-minute program. If you're wondering what in the world you'd say for 30 full minutes, relax.

It is easy to decide what to say if you've carefully crafted a free report. You already have a built-in outline and content for your radio show. Now with a full 30-minute show you can do more than just work to give away a free report, you can go for the full sale.

The mistake you may be tempted to make is that you try to make the sale in a simple 60-second spot. Just as with your classified ad, postcard, and display ads, there is not enough time or space for you to make your case to close a sale.

Use the 60-second spot to lead your prospects to a free report or some other marketing device that gives you the time you need to build a case for buying your product or service. Use the 30-minute show to make the case on the air and go right for the sale.

Far too much money is lost each year on advertising that tries to sell a prospect in too small a space or too short a time. Just look at a classified ad page in any national magazine and you'll see far too many ads trying to sell with just a mere 15-word ad. Listen to your favorite radio station and listen to the ads. How many of them are trying to get you to *buy* with a mere 30-second spot? I can promise you this is money wasted.

Look for radio stations that will sell you the airtime you want, not what fits into their schedule. If you can't get 60-second spots, there are other stations you can work with. If you can't get 30-minute spots for your radio show, keep looking.

There are more and more radio stations offering 30-minute and even 60-minute spots on their stations. Not too long ago, I cohosted one of these 60-minute shows on a large AM radio station in San Diego, California. We bought the hour each week, the same time each week, and did a show on Internet marketing.

We kept all the revenue from the ads we ran during out 60-minute show, and we were able to promote anything we wanted each week, keeping the profits from all of those sales. Look into this kind of opportunity with your local talk radio stations. It's a powerful way to build a professional practice in a very short period of time. If you have enough advertisers each week, the show won't cost you a dime and you may even make a few dollars from your advertisers.

I've consulted clients ranging from chiropractors and lawyers to CPAs and business consultants who use this format and see incredible success in just a few short months.

To make radio even more appealing to you, there is now software on the market that you can use to create professional-quality radio ads and shows. Or you can also ask the radio station to borrow an unused studio, pay an audio engineer, and record right at the radio station.

In my office, I've invested in the equipment you'd normally find in a radio studio so that I can record my own ads, shows, promos, audio CDs, and now even DVDs right in my office. This was important to me since I am recording two to three times a week as well as hosting live web casts and teleseminars that all make good use of this equipment.

You certainly don't have to go to that extent in your own office, unless, like me, you've fallen in love with the technology and realize what it can do for your business.

The more creative control you have over your advertising messages, the better they will perform. For example, audio engineers may wish to add a music overlay that is far too loud for the spot and it garbles your voice to the point of being inaudible.

While you do have a lot of say about how your ads and shows turn out, you may feel intimidated to criticize or speak your mind. Don't! It's more important that you get it your way than it is to worry about hurting somebody's feelings. In the long run, if the ad works, you'll buy more airtime and everybody at the station wins.

USING THE SAME AD IN DIFFERENT MARKETS

Radio is primarily a local market medium, although satellite radio is looming in the background and may alter the face of radio in the near future when they begin accepting paid advertising on their networks.

The good news is that you can buy radio time in any market in the nation and when you've found an advertising formula that works for you, provided you run it on a similar station format with similar demographics, the odds are very much in your favor that your ad will work in other markets.

After you've done enough testing in your local market, you can then contract with ad buyers who can help you buy radio airtime an any market, usually at a substantial discount over what you could do yourself.

The reason for the discounted pricing is that there are no high commissions to be paid to the local station's ad representatives. You will pay a commission to the broker or brokerage firm you contract with, which will be less expensive than working with a station directly.

There are also brokers you can contract with that will buy up what is known in the industry as *remnant space*. This is airspace that remains unsold for a particular day. The radio can't sell airspace for yesterday's programming day, so the station will usually take very lowball offers to sell off any and all unsold airspace.

Since this is a very fast-moving marketplace, you'll want to work with a broker who is proficient in buying and negotiating the lowest possible prices for remnant airspace. It also helps if you can provide your broker with enough of a monthly budget to secure better deals.

Having a large advertising budget is the result of having advertising that works. Money alone will *not* guarantee your success in any media. Only testing will guarantee your success.

Once you have an ad that works in any media, you can create an unlimited advertising budget to run your ad since predicting the results will become possible and fairly accurate. If you know that for every $1,000 you invest in your advertising you will bring in $1,500 or more, the only question becomes how many places can you invest your $1,000.

This is the ultimate formula for success in any advertising you do, and you'll get there faster when you use motivational marketing strategies in all your marketing efforts.

Let's look at how to use motivational marketing on television.

CHAPTER

14

Motivational Marketing: Television Advertising Strategies

To most marketers, television remains the most powerful of all marketing channels. This is easy to understand when you think about how human communication works. As I shared with you in the previous chapter, 7 percent of communication comes from our words and another 38 percent comes from our vocal quality, including tone, pace, and volume.

The remaining 55 percent actually comes from the visual cues we get by watching a person's body language. Body language plays a huge role in how we communicate, even if we are unaware of how it works.

With all of the other media, the element of body language is missing. This means that you have to work really hard to get your message across with just words or, like on the radio, with words and voice quality alone. When you shift to television, you add the largest part of the communication model, body language.

This is why television is such a powerful marketing channel and it's why there is a huge rush to now bring video to the Internet. As a marketing tool, it can't be beaten. However, for the same reasons that make television a powerful marketing channel, it's also the most difficult in which to succeed.

Let's begin by again looking at your message. If you were to run the typical 30-second television spot, you have about five lines of copy to deliver your message. While this length spot is a disaster for radio, it's common on television because you have the additional benefit of a moving picture to work with.

Instead of just having a motivational marketing headline, you're also able to couple your headline with imagery that delivers its own message to your viewers. There is an added level of complexity when working with television. Images have a vocabulary all their own and depending on what you decide to show in your commercial, you'll be sending different messages to your market.

❧ SUCCESS STRATEGY ❧

Video is fast coming to the Internet where it will be possible for a company of any size to use television-like ads on their web sites. Keep an eye on this because it is a powerful marketing tool that is now available to everybody at virtually no cost.

When you sit down to craft your television commercial, you need to think in terms of imagery as well as copy. Let's assume for a moment that you have already tested your motivational marketing headline with classified ads, postcards, in sales letters, on your web site, and maybe even on the radio. For the most part, it's been profitable for you.

Now you're ready to get your message on television.

DECIDING WHAT TO SHOW FIRST

The question of what image to show your viewer first in your ad can stump many advertisers who are new to the world of television. The initial images should seek to capture your target audience by touching them in an emotional way.

If I were to create a television ad, the first shot might be of a couple, sitting on the beach in paradise, with an opening line something to the effect of "Have you been dreaming about owning a business that would allow you to vacation in paradise anytime you'd like?"

You can see that I've coupled the voice message to the images you'll see in the initial part of the ad. Your goal here is to make sure the opening image does two things. First, it *must* stop your viewer in their tracks. Chances are your viewer has been waiting for a commercial break to jump up and run to the restroom, so your ad has to be more important to them then a trip to the restroom.

Next, the opening line you choose (your headline) has to be in perfect alignment with the images you're showing. This is the one-two punch most television ads miss.

Far too many television commercials are produced for free by the television stations that are all-too-eager to collect your advertising dollars when they air your ad. They are usually created by people who know how to operate a video camera and wire a microphone, but who have no knowledge of marketing, much less motivational marketing.

As with any print or radio advertising, it's best that you choose not to use the free services offered by the television stations or cable networks selling you the ad space. A better approach is to act as the producer of your own television commercial and hire a production team who will do as you ask them to do, without question.

You should be the one to sit in the editing room, deciding what shots to use, when to start them, and when to change to a new shot. It's easy to say that you're just not skilled enough to produce your commercial, but if you leave it to somebody else, you're going to have to live with what they give you.

I've had many clients who sat in on the editing process and, because they were not technical, they saw things the technical person did not see. At the end of the process, the resulting commercial was much better than it would have otherwise been. And more important, it worked.

If you're not skilled in the area of television production, you might even be more valuable as part of the production because you see television from a viewer's perspective. There is no more powerful position than being able to place yourself in the role of the viewer who will ultimately see your ad.

As marketers, sometimes we miss this fact because we are caught up in the technical issues of creating and designing our marketing programs. To get around this issue, I've actually cut out and pasted my ad mock-ups into pages of the publications I'm going to run them in just to see how they look in print.

You can do the same with your television commercial. Record a few minutes of the television station you're using to run your ad and have your production crew cut in your ad. Then, play it back viewing it as you would if you were at home watching your television.

This process can tell you a lot about your ad and how to further improve it so that it works. This is called seeing your ad *in context* and very few marketers ever consider doing this.

After viewing ads in context, I often make changes to the ads so that they stand out more from the noise of the other ads. This has resulted in dramatically improved results.

The entire motivational marketing concept is based on putting yourself in the shoes of those you're attempting to persuade and doing all you can to capture their attention and motivate them to respond. It makes no sense to throw your ads out there and "see what happens" when you've come this far already.

Take the time, invest the money, and look at your ads in context. If you're doing direct mail, send a sample of your mailing piece to yourself. It will make a huge difference when you actually open up your mailbox. You may find that you didn't even notice your mailing piece was in your stack of mail and that may mean you want to make it a little bolder or brighter so it stands out.

Your television commercial may need to be louder, brighter, or have music that is more upbeat. You might not notice these elements when you're looking at your commercial on a monitor in an editing suite, but they will jump out at you when you see your ad in context.

Using television to promote your products or services can be somewhat more targeted than when using radio. With the advent of the dozens and dozens of new cable-only stations, you can narrow down your market, usually much better than is currently possible with radio.

If you're looking for a business-oriented audience, there are many news stations and financial stations that attract a primarily business-oriented audience. There are networks that reach younger audiences, women, mothers, sports fans, and the list goes on and on.

This is important for you as the advertiser since you'll be looking to segment your market as much as possible to get the most response from your advertising efforts. While it's a neat idea to think you want to reach everybody who watches television, "everybody" is not your market and it's the first clue that you have not done your homework.

The tighter you can be with targeting the correct prospects, the farther your advertising dollars will go.

RESPONSE TO YOUR TELEVISION AD

It is important to consider the ways in which people will be able to respond to your television ad. Through many years of testing, I've yet to find a better option than offering your viewers a toll-free number that they can call 24 hours a day, every day.

It's tempting to drive response to a web site (not to mention cheaper), but you'll lose many folks who would rather pick up the phone and speak with a live person. Remember, for decades advertisers have trained viewers to respond now by calling a toll-free number, so this is what will work best for you.

If you want to include a web site for prospects to visit, make sure the domain name is radio friendly. Again, viewers are not sitting by their television; pen in hand ready to write down your web address. It has to be simple, memorable, and preferably short.

However, your viewers are closer to a telephone, pen, and paper at home than they are listening to the radio in their cars. Thus, you can run your television ad fewer times to get a better level of response than you would typically get on the radio using the same number of airings of your ad.

Frequency is still important when running your television ads. People do need to see your ad several times, so you'll want to be sure to negotiate a contract that will allow your ad to run at the same, or very close to the same time each day.

If you choose to run your ad during a particular show because you know the audience for this show closely matches your preferred market, your best bet would be to run your television ad only during this show every time the show airs.

Compare this to what the television station may want to sell you, which is one spot here, another there, all at random times, during different shows. The station is interested in filling the unsold airtime as best they can. They are rarely excited about an advertiser who wants to run the same ad at the same time on the same station day after day.

Think of what this looks like from the viewer's perspective. She is already trained to tune into her favorite show at a certain time each day, or each week. If you place the same commercial on the air of that channel during that same show, how does the viewer perceive your company?

The viewer will see you as being much bigger than you are because in her mind, you are "all over" the television airwaves. Actually, you're only on one channel at the same time each day, but since few people watch the same station all day long, it appears as if you're on the air all the time.

This is a huge motivator when it comes to building trust in your business. The more often you appear on the air, the bigger and more trustworthy you will appear to your prospects.

It's a test of your will to get the station to agree to such an arrangement. They will tell you it's better to hit multiple audiences, once here, another time there, because you never know who is watching.

That is great if you have the budget to run multiple ads on multiple stations, but rarely is that the case. You're much better off running on the same station at the same time each day. The consistency will bring more response during your on-air campaign.

MOTIVATIONAL TELEVISION

One powerful strategy, which far too few television advertisers use, is to give away something free to generate a fresh prospect for their business. As in all other media, advertisers are lulled into believing that in 30 seconds, with just five lines of copy, they can close a sale on television.

This just isn't how it works! You'll be much better off if you'll tap into the emotional motivator of getting something for free, and make that offer in your television spot. Let me share an example from one of my own clients of how powerful this might be for you.

One of my favorite clients owned a boat dealership that at the time had a single location and was doing about $850,000 a year in sales. This is not bad by most standards, but the owner wanted to tap into the world of television to build the business even more.

As you might expect, the advertising sales representative from the cable company did a nice job of selling him a full schedule of ads. You guessed it, they were all over the place in terms of time of day and the stations they would run on. One ad here at 8:00 A.M., another there at 4:00 P.M., then a few overnight ads. The schedule was a mess. The cable system needed to plug open holes, so they sold my client hard, and he bought it all.

The problem we faced was that you couldn't sell a boat in 30 seconds. But that's not what the ad rep told my client. The rep went so far as to tell him, "They sell cars, boats, houses, and more with these kinds of television spots. This is television, you can sell anything!"

I would be hard-pressed to sell you a candy bar in 30 seconds, forget about a $30,000+ boat. The ad rep was likely referring to the old saying that you have to build your brand, and that takes lots of advertising that will someday result in a sale, maybe.

Don't buy it. As an entrepreneur, you do not have the time or money to try and build a brand, you need sales and you need them yesterday. My client was this type of entrepreneur. He needed and wanted more business; he did not want to build a brand.

So how do you sell a boat on television in 30 seconds? You could give the boats away for free, and you might get one or two curious souls to stop by to see if it was for real, but you can't sell in that time frame.

Knowing that, I suggested to my client that we instead create a 30-minute show where we could hit on all the emotional motivators several times. He was skeptical because he had just heard his sales rep tell him that he could sell a boat on television in 30 seconds. Now I was telling him to create a 30-minute show instead.

I both produced and directed the 30-minute show, and we shot it in a single day. What we did next was something that you should do in your own business. While we now had a full 30-minute show that we could put on the air, that wasn't the plan.

Instead, I chose to use the 30-second spots he had already purchased to give away VHS videotapes of the 30-minute show. Follow me here because this is important. When you give something away for free, a 30-second spot is really all you need.

We aired a simple 30-second spot that offered a free video on "How to Buy Your New Boat." The catch was that to get a copy, you had to stop by the dealership and a representative would happily hand you a free copy of the tape that was valued at $24.95.

At the same time, the dealership also got your name, address, and telephone number so they could follow up with you at a later time. It didn't take long to prove you could sell a boat with a 30-second spot, a free videotape, and a 30-minute show.

In the next three years, this dealership went from an $850,000-per-year dealership in one location to a $9-million-per-year dealership with four locations. This happened because we figured out how to correctly use emotional motivators in both the 30-second spot and in the 30-minute show.

The resulting sales required little or no selling, arm-twisting, hard negotiation, or other forms of manipulation. People who had seen the 30-minute show came into the dealership ready to buy.

This strategy is no different from the many others I've already shared with you in this book. Offer something free with your front-end advertising. Then use that free item to do the heavy lifting to make the sale.

We used the 30-second spot with the emotional motivator of getting something for free and making your dream of owning a new boat come true. We used the 30-minute VHS videotape to literally sell you the boat, emotionally.

I could write a whole other book on how to craft these give-away items so that they sell for you, but there are already quite a few great books on the topic.

If you do decide to create a 30-minute show, you'll have plenty of time to hit all five emotional motivators during your show. I recommend you spend a lot of time creating your show so that you hit all five emotional motivators repeatedly.

A good exercise is to sit down in front of your television and watch some late-night infomercials. Yes, I know you wouldn't be caught dead watching them, but they do represent some of the best efforts in television marketing. Look for shows that air night after night, and shows that have been on the air for years.

These repeated shows are working and are worth studying. Try and find how they used the five emotional motivators in their show. If you look, you'll see plenty of evidence of motivational marketing in practice.

However, you may want to hide your credit cards before you start watching infomercials. Your desire to buy that next piece of exercise equipment is sure evidence that the marketers behind the show have dialed into your emotional motivators and have hit them repeatedly during their show.

These are the shows I record and put away to study for my next television production. If they can get me excited, I know I can learn from them, and so can you.

These shows typically cost hundreds of thousands of dollars to produce and test, so when you finally put them on the air, you know they have been fine-tuned and are producing profitable results. They will not stay on the air very long if they fail to produce results.

❧ SUCCESS STRATEGY ❧

Watching infomercials that are already on the air is the best education you can get prior to going into the studio to produce your own television show. Get into the habit of watching these marketing masterpieces as time allows.

Airtime can be costly, but if used correctly, television is a powerful marketing tool that allows you fully exploit the power of motivational marketing in many ways. Although it's not the media to start with, it should be on your list of marketing channels to use as you build your business and find the message(s) that really motivate your prospects to respond.

Get Out There and Motivate Your Prospects

Congratulations! You've made it this far into the world of motivational marketing. That's the good news. The bad news might be that everything you've read up to this point won't be worth an extra dime in profit to your business.

How can that be? How can I spend 14 chapters sharing ideas on motivational marketing, but now say it won't amount to anything? This is the unfortunate outcome of far too many business owners who have been exposed to this and other marketing strategies.

Most people will not get out there and motivate their prospects, which is the most important step in making motivational marketing work for them. They will have every excuse in the book for not taking this step. They will have spent their time reading this book, taking notes, agreeing with most everything they've read, but end up doing nothing with it.

Here's a simple analogy for my role in your life at this point. I'm just like a waiter in a restaurant. Your waiter comes to your table, asks you what you want to eat, places your order with the kitchen, and returns shortly thereafter with your meal.

A waiter can place a napkin on your lap, crack some fresh pepper onto your salad, refresh your cup of coffee, and ask you if you need anything more. But that's it. He can't do much more for you after he has delivered what you requested to your table.

This next step will make all the difference in your business. Just having a plate of food placed in front you is not going to quell your hunger pains. You have to pick up that fork and use it to put food in your mouth!

Like your waiter, I can't use the fork for you. Although there are many times when I'd like to pick up that fork full of food and cram it into my client's mouth, I know I can't do that. My job ends at this point because I have to pass the next step over to you.

You now have in your hands the same tools that many of the largest and most successful companies use in every ad, on every phone call, in every sales letter, and in every marketing piece they use to drive sales.

In the pages of this powerful book, I left nothing out. You bought this book expecting to have effective marketing tools you could turn into profit in a very short period of time, and I committed myself to living up to your expectation. If you love what you read in this book, the odds are then very high that you'll tell your family, friends, and business associates and they too will buy a copy of this book.

Included in this book are many marketing strategies that you can put into use immediately in your business. This is a book that you will want to keep handy as you create new marketing materials for your business.

Thus, the next step separates the winners from those who want to be winners. This step creates success in your business beyond your wildest dreams and makes all the difference.

The next step, once you start it, keeps going for the lifetime of your business. Once you begin to experience the power of motivational marketing in your business, nothing else will ever be good enough again.

Your business can and will take a definite step forward the moment you begin this next step. And the catch here is that nobody can take this step for you, at least not initially. You are the one who read this book; you've seen the ways to apply motivational marketing to your business, and by now, you're motivated to do something with this information.

YOUR NEXT STEP

The next logical step is to turn the information and strategies in this book into profit for you. There is no point in reading this book and then putting it up on your shelf where it will become just another shelf-help book. It's time to use what you've been given in a way that will produce real, measurable profits for you.

Pick just one thing to begin with to avoid what happens with most business owners who try to take it all on at once. They get overwhelmed and instead of creating more success, they end up creating chaos for themselves.

The trick to making things work is to take one step at a time. Review the previous chapters and pick out just one motivational marketing strategy that you can easily incorporate into your marketing. It could be something rather simple like changing one word in your headline or something bigger such as creating a new ad using several of the emotional motivators.

Stick with this one thing until it's complete—which is *not* an easy task. Some business owners or entrepreneurs have a hard time staying focused on any one project for more than five minutes at a time; they love to have lots of stuff going on and love to push their energy in many different directions at once.

While this is good for an adrenaline rush, it's not the pathway to creating successful marketing systems that guarantee financial success. Instead, follow through on even the smallest of ideas, one after another and soon you'll be creating the critical momentum that propels you to success.

To get started, write down the first idea that comes to mind when you think of motivational marketing and how it applies to your business.

For many people, running a simple classified ad is a great first step. You can get an ad done inside of an hour and have it on its way to be published in just a few minutes.

Then, you can start to look at the other marketing pieces you've either already created or were planning to create and see how you can integrate motivational marketing into those pieces. Start with pieces you know you can afford to run because there is no point to working on a television commercial if your budget cannot support buying television airtime.

You may look at your web site and see what parts of it you can transform with motivational marketing. Or maybe you have a postcard that could use an update and you see a way to use a motivational marketing headline to spruce it up.

Look at everything you're doing to promote your business and when you do, ask yourself if you can use motivational marketing to enhance, improve, or completely recreate what you're doing.

You have to act on what you've read throughout the pages of this book. Far too often, many great ideas, potentially very profitable business ideas, and businesses that could be making a difference are just barely keeping their doors open because their owners know what to do, but fail to do it.

This book will be read by tens of thousands of business owners around the world. The information in this book can help just about any business grow exponentially. But I'm just like the waiter. I've brought you the information, the answers, and the strategies, now it's up to you to pick them up and put them into action in your business.

The good part is that very little of what I've shared with you in this book is really all that complicated to do, and even with the smallest budget for advertising you can still use motivational marketing.

A few years back, a man attended one of my live seminars and listened intently to what I had to share on the topic of motivational marketing. He was motivated to put everything he had heard into play in his brand new business. The challenge was that he only had a very small amount of money to invest in his advertising. I gave him the following advice: get other people to pay for your advertising.

❦ SUCCESS STRATEGY ❦

If your success is dependent only on the amount of money you are able to invest to promote your business, you're only going to be able to grow by so much each year. Always look for ways to promote your business using other people's money.

GET OTHER PEOPLE TO PAY FOR YOUR ADVERTISING

Using other people's money to pay for your advertising wipes out the most common excuse for not using motivational marketing in your business. This strategy is rather unique and it gives you an immediate budget for advertising. I could fill another book with variations on this strategy alone.

The idea behind using other people's money to advertise your business is not a new idea. It's been done by businesses of all sizes for decades and is becoming even more popular among the Fortune 500 companies. You'll see this strategy in use on television and radio, in magazines and newspapers, and most commonly, on the Internet.

The strategy is based on the understanding that advertising works best when it's used to generate leads. When a lead is generated, that lead can be shared among companies that are not in direct competition with one another, but that sell to the same type of prospects.

An example of this might be an Internet service provider who sells Internet access into a specific market sharing the leads they generate with a company that offers web design services and another company that offers web-hosting services.

An offline example might be a retail store that sells women's shoes sharing the leads they generate with a neighboring store that sells women's fashion clothing. They could further combine their efforts and create specific outfits that include clothing from one store and shoes from another.

The idea is that a person will buy more than one item, and the idea that you want exclusive leads is nice thought, but in reality, your exclusive lead is being bombarded everyday with thousands of marketing messages. Some of those messages may even be from your competitors.

The strategy for marketing with other people's money is simple to understand and takes a little legwork to put into play, but it could result in having a virtually unlimited advertising budget without investing a dime of your own money.

Here's how it works. First, you identify the primary market you want to reach in as specific a way as possible. You should be laser focused on a core group of people that you know want what you have to offer.

Second, identify a dozen or so other companies that also sell to this same primary market, but that do not directly compete with you. If you sell legal services, you may not want to partner with another attorney who offers the same legal services as you.

However, if your law practice focuses on estate planning or asset protection, you could partner with another attorney who practices real estate law. They are closely related but not directly competitive.

In my business, I target business owners because there is absolutely no shortage of businesses that I can partner with to share leads. The question to ask is, "Who is already selling to the prospects I want to reach?"

Here are some examples of companies that sell to business owners:

- ✔ Internet service providers.
- ✔ Office supply catalogs and retailers.
- ✔ Merchant account providers.
- ✔ Computer vendors.
- ✔ Insurance companies.
- ✔ Attorneys and accountants.
- ✔ Coaches and consultants.
- ✔ Information marketers.
- ✔ Telephone companies, including cell phones.
- ✔ Software companies.

The idea is to build a list of the types of companies that already sell to the people you want to reach. After you create your list, you can pick a category and start listing companies by name that you might partner with.

The next step will require some legwork, but with a little creativity, you can make this step painless. You might create a simple one-page proposal outlining your advertising plan and your intention to share leads with your partners.

This works because for just a small portion of what it would normally cost to run an ad, all the advertisers can reap the benefit of getting every single lead generated by a shared advertising campaign.

Since your partners are not competitors, sharing all the leads will not pose a problem. It's completely legal to do this, and the entire direct marketing industry would have a hard time existing if this practice were not common.

On the Internet, you can legally share the leads you generate as long as you have this information clearly stated in your web site's privacy policy. If you say you'll never share your list with anybody and you do, then you'll have problems. If you say you could share your list, as most corporations today do all the time, you're fine.

With the available technology today, it's not that difficult to automate the entire lead-sharing system. You could set up an auto-responder system that is designed to send each of your partners a copy of the leads the moment they are generated on a web site. I have found the best system to use, and you can get it here: www.UltimateWealth.com/cart.htm.

On the money side of things, what you might do is call up the representative for the media you're considering for your advertising campaign. If you were going to buy time on television, for instance, contact your local cable company or go to the station directly if it's a local station.

Your goal here is to find out how much you'll need to raise in order to run your advertising the way you want it run. If you find out you need $10,000 for instance, but you're just getting started and don't have the money, don't worry.

Divide that number by 10. Now all you need to do is find 10 advertising partners with whom you will share 100 percent of the leads generated from your advertising. Each partner can participate for just $1,000.

If the 10 companies were to go to the television station, each one would have to pay $10,000 for the exact same advertising schedule they can share with you for just $1,000. And they get all the leads, just as before.

The downside is that they don't get a say on the ad that runs, and they have to share the leads with you and 10 other businesses. These are not issues when you compare them to the price for the airtime or ad space. It's a bargain. And a bargain is an emotional motivator. A powerful emotional motivator you can easily use to enroll your advertising partners.

A LEAD-GENERATING ADVERTISEMENT

I've covered this elsewhere in this book, but I wanted to share it again in context of using other people's money to advertise. It would make sense that if you used other people's money to promote your business, you'd have a harder time getting partners to join you.

A better method is to create advertising that is designed to generate leads. You'll do this by using the emotional motivator of getting something for free. Your ad will offer a free report, a free audio CD, a free e-book, or special report. The title of this information product giveaway will act as the filter that will only bring you the kind of prospects you want most.

For years, I've given away an e-book called, "Internet Marketing Secrets" on my web site. I've used all forms of advertising to give away tens of thousands of copies of this e-book. The title is what brought me the type of prospects I could then sell to later on.

A person who has no interest in selling on the Internet will likely *not* be interested in my e-book even if I attached a $100 bill to the front cover. However, the person I want to attract, the person who wants to know how to market on the Internet, will eagerly respond to my offer for this e-book.

Narrow your title so that it doesn't attract everybody, but do not make it so narrow that it is of no value to your advertising partners. Do this right and you'll never have to invest a penny of your own money in advertising. You'll have plenty of advertising partners willing to buy advertising at a discount.

TESTING MAKES ALL THE DIFFERENCE

Successful marketing is truly based on one core principle that is commonly overlooked by business owners, yet this practice makes the biggest difference by a landslide in terms of results. The concept is *testing*.

Whenever you see an ad that catches your attention, the chances are great that the ad was not the result of somebody sitting at a computer for 15 minutes, whipping something up, and sending it off to be published. The ad has likely been tested in many publications and undergone many changes before appearing in the publication. While it is technically possible to create an ad that is a hit on the first try, the odds are stacked terribly high against you.

To be successful, you have to get used to the fact that testing is going to be an integral part of your success formula. Testing can be frustrating, time-consuming, and a drag to do. Testing is also the fastest way for you to consistently hit advertising home runs.

While I have seen people pull off a literal miracle with an untested ad, the vast majority of businesses that play this game fail miserably. The issue we're faced with is simply this; no matter how much marketing experience you have, no matter how many ads you've already created, no matter how great a copywriter you are, the only way you're really ever going to know if what you've created will work is by putting it in front of your audience.

Your audience will either respond or they won't. This is all part of the testing process to find out what your audience will respond to and to refine it until the number of people responding is high enough to grow your business year after year.

This is the true secret to success in marketing. Apply it with your motivational marketing efforts and you have a formula for success you can use with any business.

16

Concluding Thoughts on Motivational Marketing

Although there are many things in life that you are told not to do, motivational marketing is something you *must* do. It's very low risk and has a very high return when executed properly.

Motivational marketing will help you reach the dreams that got you into your business in the first place and help persuade many more prospects into seeing why they must buy what you're selling right now.

Motivational marketing will help you dominate your market while your competitors are still out there with ads that barely work. You'll see double, triple, and even quadruple the response to your advertising efforts when compared with competitors who advertise in the same publications offering the same products and services.

This increased response will allow you to do more business than your competitors. I would even go so far as to suggest that using motivational marketing could make your competitors a non-issue for you in the very near term.

If you're not yet sold on adding motivational marketing to your business, you may want to give it a test with your next marketing effort. Think about your prospects and what will help them respond to your message emotionally, then use that emotion in your marketing.

You may simply shift your thinking from what you already know about marketing to what you've been shown in this book. When you stop thinking about what you're selling in terms of color, shape, size, and price and begin instead to think about how it makes your customers feel, you'll be on the right track.

This shift in thinking, when it occurs, will change much more in your business than just what you say in your advertising. It will change the way you, or your employees, answer the telephone, how you reply to e-mail messages, how you write thank-you letters to your best clients, what you say in speeches, and so on.

When you learn the power of tapping into people's emotional wants instead of what you think they need, everything will change in your business.

To successfully make this shift in thinking, you have to begin asking questions. Start by asking questions of your best customers. Find out why they buy from you and what makes them choose you over the competition.

Listen for words that reflect the emotional motivators. If your customers tell you that because of your product they are now able to be, do, or have things they never thought possible, write these things down. It's easy to gloss over them in your mind because they are not the concrete answers you've been trained to seek out. Your customers want to share how doing business with you really makes them feel. It's simply up to you to listen. Listen to what makes them excited about working with you. Listen to the emotional charge they get from doing business with you.

If you are having a hard time getting this kind of information, you may need to do some deeper research. There is no product on the market today that does not engage the buyer emotionally. Yes, even buying a box of nails evokes emotion—the emotion of seeing a project completed be it hanging a picture or building a new house. Some emotions are subtle and may be hard to see, but they are indeed there.

The last time I drove by a Wal-Mart store, I thought about the emotions their customers feel as they buy billions and billions of dollars of products. Clearly, Wal-Mart's calling card is price based, and their primary emotional motivator is that of getting a bargain.

What is it for your business? What keeps your customers coming back to you repeatedly? What gets them in the door the first time?

There is absolutely no shortage of companies that use the power of emotion to drive sales. Name any industry, and you'll find hundreds of companies who are actively using emotion to motivate their prospects to buy.

THE FINAL WORD

The last thing I have to share with you as we close this chapter of our relationship together is simply this; you deserve to achieve success in your life even beyond what you may think is possible today. The temptation may be, as you begin to see more and more success, to "hit the brakes" to slow things down. This is a normal reaction to sudden bursts of incredible success. You can overcome this reaction in many ways so that your business continues to grow.

One way that I have used successfully is to visualize myself at the helm of my business, as it is today, and as it would be at 30 percent larger than it is today. Once I begin to feel comfortable with that image, I'll visualize my business at 50 percent larger than it is today.

Repeat this process until you can clearly see your business at 500 percent of what it is today and feel comfortable with that vision. If you start to grow your business and are not completely comfortable with how things start to look, you'll simply end up applying the brakes and the growth will stop.

Many business owners experience this during their careers. To avoid a slow down, visualize your success before it actually happens. You'll be in a much better position to accept success when you begin using motivational marketing in your business and it begins to really work for you.

I'd like to thank you for investing your time in reading this book, and I hope that we will soon meet in person. Maybe we'll meet at one of my live seminars, or maybe you'll participate in a live webcast or teleseminar with me. Or maybe you'll become one of my prized consulting clients and see your business rocket to the top in almost no time.

I would be interested to know of your progress with motivational marketing. Who knows, we could end up being on a television show together someday.

I wish you success beyond your wildest dreams with *Motivational Marketing*.

Until we meet again, be outstanding!

ROBERT IMBRIALE
"The Motivational Marketer"
www.MotivationalMarketing.com

Important Motivational
—— Marketing Resources ——

www.MotivationalMarketing.com
This is the official resource site for this book where you'll find additional motivational marketing articles, tools, strategies, events, and more. Be sure to go here to collect your free motivational marketing gifts and much more!

www.EffortlessMarketingCourse.com
This is a free e-book on how to harness the power of effortless marketing using the power of motivational marketing. This is the only full course currently available that shows you how to put motivational marketing to work for you on the Internet.

How to Think, Act, and Become a Millionaire
This is a free mini-course on CD. Get your copy now at www. UltimateWealth.com.

www.RobertImbriale.com
This site gives more information about the author and his availability for speaking engagements, consulting, interviews, and more.

www.UltimateWealth.com
This web site offers articles, audio and video programs, seminars, and more for all kinds of businesses. This is the author's main

marketing web site and is a great site to study for additional motivational marketing ideas.

www.TheNextMillionaire.com
Powerful training programs for business owners on how to become a millionaire in your own business. Check this site for free resources, upcoming events, live web casts, and free teleseminars.

www.UltimateWealth.tv
Weekly live web casts, recorded video presentations, and more are waiting for you on this web site. Many are available free for you to view over the Internet immediately.

www.UltimateWebProfits.com
This is a free e-course on how to become an Internet millionaire. This course will show several strategies for successfully marketing your business over the Internet.

www.NoBSWebMarketing.com
This is a free trial subscription to Dan Kennedy's *No B.S. Marketing Letter.* Get three free months of the newsletter to try. Cancel anytime.

INDEX